Dictionary of Shipping Terms and Phrases

Edward F Steven

FICS, FCIS

Author of "Shipping Practice

GW01066203

Pitman Publishing

Second edition 1971
First paperback edition 1971

SIR ISAAC PITMAN AND SONS LTD
Pitman House, Parker Street, Kingsway, London WC2B 5PB
PO Box 6038, Portal Street, Nairobi, Kenya

SIR ISAAC PITMAN (AUST) PTY LTD
Pitman House, Bouverie Street, Carlton, Victoria 3053, Australia

PITMAN PUBLISHING COMPANY SA LTD
PO Box 11231, Johannesburg, South Africa

PITMAN PUBLISHING CORPORATION
6 East 43rd Street, New York, NY 10017, USA

SIR ISAAC PITMAN (CANADA) LTD
Pitman House, 381–383 Church Street, Toronto 3, Canada

THE COPP CLARK PUBLISHING COMPANY
517 Wellington Street, Toronto 2B, Canada

Cased edition ISBN: 0 273 36038 8
Paperback edition ISBN: 0 273 36039 6

Made in Great Britain at the Pitman Press, Bath
G1—(B437/B1040)

Preface

THIS little volume of Shipping Terms is offered for ready reference. Stereotyped wording has been departed from where it has been possible to give a clearer meaning in other phraseology.

It is hoped that it will be of help both to the student preparing for examinations and to the man in the Industry during the course of his business.

Due acknowledgment is made to Mr C S J Butterfield FICS, AIArb, for his most helpful co-operation.

For the benefit of future editions the author would appreciate the kind assistance of readers who may feel that other useful shipping phrases, within their knowledge, could be included in this little dictionary.

A

A.1. Classification which is granted by Lloyd's Register relative to the condition of the ship. Classification may be described as comparison with an ideal, each classification society having its own standards of what may be considered an ideal ship.

100 A.1. is the cypher adopted by *Lloyd's Register* 100 A., referring to ship, 1 referring to equipment. Varying degrees of class, *e.g.* 90 A.1., 80 A.2., etc., have long since been discontinued. The present classifications are:—" ✠ 100 A.1." which is assigned to steel vessels built in accordance with the Society's rules, and having the scantlings set forth in the tables appropriate to the maximum draught permitted by the dimensions. " ✠ 100 A.1. With Freeboard " which is assigned to vessels built in accordance with the rules and the scantlings set forth in the tables appropriate to the draught which is less than the maximum draught permitted by the dimensions.

A.A. Certificate that the crew has been engaged before a Superintendent of the Mercantile Marine, and the Officers' and Master's certificates required by the Board of Trade have been examined.

a.a. Always afloat. A term to be found in charter parties, which provides, that at all times, and at all stages of the tide, the ship must remain afloat. It is, therefore, an obligation imposed by the shipowner that the charterer shall select a berth at which the vessel may load or unload with a sufficient water depth. The principal factor is the protection of the ship's hull against hard substances lying submerged in the port or river-bed.

a.a.r. Against all risks. Goods may be insured against "all risks," but such a term has definite limited meaning. Whilst the term covers perils which are generally accepted, it must not be extended beyond this. All insurances on an "all risk" basis are subject to the Memorandum (final clause in policy).

A.B. A seaman who has served three years at sea and is certified as efficient (Sec. 58, M.S. Act).

Abandonment. The giving up of control over a vessel when she is in the position of a constructive total loss. Where a claim is submitted to underwriters in respect of a loss, the Notice of Abandonment (q.v.) must be given.

Abeam. In a line at right angles to the vessel's length. Opposite the centre of the vessel's side.

ab initio. From the beginning.

Act of God. Any fortuituous act which could not have been prevented by any amount of human care and forethought. The expression should not be deemed to cover incidents which are normally described in everyday life as such, but only such acts which come within the above description. It may be suggested that it is always possible to prevent such a loss by refusing to let the ship sail, which argument is logically correct. But restrictive conditions upon the employment of the ship in its legitimate trade and purpose are not acceptable as a disclaimer of an approved Act of God.

Act of War. This expression covers any act of war, whether it involves belligerents or neutrals.

Actual Total Loss (A.T.L). A total loss in a marine adventure is adjudged by marine insurance to be either an actual total loss or a constructive total loss (q.v.). Where the subject matter insured is destroyed, or so damaged as to cease to be a thing of the kind insured, or where the assured is irretrievably deprived thereof, then there is an actual total loss.

Additional Premium. See **A/P.**

Address Commission. A commission paid to the charterer's agent who arranges the loading of the vessel, and is usually based on gross freight.

Admiralty Measured Mile. A mile of 6080 feet.

Ad Val. Ad valorem. Phrase meaning " according to the value," used in many ways where quotations, insurance rates, and rates of freight are made. The expression also appears in connection with Customs Duties, many of which are assessable on the valuation of goods.

Ad valorem duty. A duty based upon the value of the goods.

Ad valorem freight. Freight which is charged upon the value of the goods, and not upon weight or measurement.

Advance Notes. Drafts upon the owners of the vessel, or other employer of crew, for an advance of wages. An advance note is given, if required, to the seaman upon signing articles, and is exchangeable with a marine storeman or dealer who, in turn, presents it to the shipping company for payment. The note is honoured by the shipping company, usually within three days of the sailing of the vessel, provided the seaman was on board. If the seaman fails to join the ship, the advance note becomes void.

a.f.—Advance Freight. Freight paid in advance, either in exchange for documents or at such other time as may be stipulated in the contract. Although freight becomes due only when the goods are safely carried and are ready to be delivered, the shipowner, by stipulating advance freight, makes this a condition of his contract, and it is therefore enforceable. When advance freight is paid it is deemed earned on payment, and is not recoverable, ship lost or not lost, unless the loss is due to the fault or privity of the shipowner. Contracts worded in such a manner as to indicate that the advance payment is on account of disbursements, or payment for the provision of funds to the master, do not fall within the interpretation of advance freight.

Affreightment. Contracts of affreightment are for the carriage of goods by sea and may be expressed in a charter party, or by an agreement which is evidenced by the terms and conditions of the bill of lading.

Against All Risks. See a.a.r.

Aground. A vessel is aground when it touches bottom. It is recognized that there should be an actual grounding, and not merely a slight touch, as when a ship passes over a sand bar. Although no specified time or duration of the grounding has ever been named, there must be some time, if even of the briefest moment, to justify the use of the term.

A/H. Abbreviation used in chartering to indicate Antwerp —Hamburg range of ports, i.e. Antwerp, and/or Hamburg and any port between those two places.

Allotment. The allocation of a part of his wages by the seaman to any person as prescribed by B.o.T. regulations, to be paid monthly or halfmonthly (or at such other time as may be agreed). The total amounts so paid out are calculated and deducted from total wages upon the termination of agreement.

All Risks Whatsoever. Covers more than all risks (all marine risks) but some casualty must occur before a recoverable claim can arise. This is a slightly more comprehensive term than "all risks" which generally only covers specified risks.

Always afloat. See **a.a.**

American Bureau of Shipping. American Ship Classification Society.

Amidships. The centre of the vessel's length or breadth.

Ante bellum. Pre-war.

A/P. Additional premium. An extra premium charged to cover an increase of the insurance, or to cover additional risks, e.g. " change of voyage."

Apparent good order and condition. The statement relative to the condition of the goods which have been shipped, and are so described on the bill of lading. The shipowner, having no right of inspection of contents, receives goods and acknowledges receipt only according to their external condition. If a bill is issued with this statement unqualified, it is said to be a "clean bill" (q.v.). Qualifications (*e.g.* "case stained," "unprotected," etc.) make the bill "dirty" (q.v.).

Appendix. One of the four volumes of *Lloyd's Register*.

A.R. All risks. All marine risks (*Vale & Co.* and *Van Appen*, 1921)—see **a.a.r.** (Against all risks).

Arbitration. The process of submitting matters of dispute, or of a controversial nature, to the judgment of an agreed independent person or persons, without applying to the courts for a settlement. Arbitration is now regulated by the Arbitration Act, 1950, and the decision of the arbitrator, is, if correctly given, enforceable at law. It is normal for all bills of lading and charter parties to include an arbitration clause for the settlement of disputes.

Arbitration Award. The decision given by arbitrators after hearing a dispute. Such a decision if given correctly in accordance with law is binding upon the parties and any failure to comply with an arbitrator's finding amounts to contempt of court.

Arrest. Detention of a vessel with a view to her ultimate release when the purpose of her arrest has been fulfilled. An arrest may take place when a ship has contravened some port or national regulation, or when the ship is held during the process of exercise of a maritime lien.

Arrived Ship. A vessel conforms with this expression when she has arrived at the agreed place of loading (or discharge), is ready in all respects to load (or discharge), and notice of readiness has been given within the prescribed times. All these conditions must be fulfilled before the vessel can be called an arrived ship.

A/S. Account Sales. An agent's account of sales, etc., submitted to the exporter.

As fast as can. In the loading or discharge of a ship it is the obligation of the charterer to supply the cargo to the ship as fast as she can load it, this condition is limited by the recognized handling capacity of the port. If the daily figure is, say, 1,000 tons, the supply of that quantity would meet the obligation in spite of the fact that the ship could load, say, 1,200 tons. See also **f.a.c.**

As near thereto as she can safely get. Qualifying condition to a named port or place of discharge. A vessel may be prevented from entering port of discharge and has the right to move to nearest other discharging point. This may be a port some considerable distance away. The cause of prevention should be ascertained and if the reason is of a temporary nature the vessel should wait. If permanent, then the ship may take the necessary action.

Assignee. Person who has rights assigned to him.

Assignment. The written document by which goods or property are transferred.

Assignor. Person who makes the assignment.

At and From. A marine insurance term which covers insurance while the vessel is at a specified port as well as for the voyage therefrom.

Austral. Chamber of Shipping 1928 Australian Grain Charter Party form.

Austwheat. Australian Grain Charter Party 1956.

Average. A loss, e.g. General Average—general loss, or Particular Average—particular loss. See **G.A.** and **P.A.**

Average Adjuster. An average adjuster is an authority on all aspects of marine insurance law and loss adjustments. He is the expert who assesses the losses and contributions under a general average act (q.v.).

Average Bond. The guarantee given by a receiver of cargo that he will pay his contribution to the general average fund when settlement is finally made. Such a bond is given on a recognized standard form (*e.g.* Lloyd's Average Bond) and is counter-signed by the consignee's bankers or other guarantor.

Awash. Level with the surface of the water.

Azcon. Chamber of Shipping Grain Charter Party 1910 for Azoff Berth Contracts.

B

Backfreight. Freight which is charged for the return of goods. The return may be due to the refusal of goods by consignee, or for the return of cargo due to over-carriage. The person responsible for over-carriage is liable to pay freight. Over-carriage may arise through wrong port marking of case (Shipper's responsibility) or overstowage of the cargo (Shipowner's error).

Back Letter. Term applied to a letter of indemnity which is given in exchange for clean bills of lading (q.v.).

Bailee. A person to whom goods or property are entrusted for a specific purpose. The contract of affreightment is one of bailment, whereby the shipowner or his agent has the care of the cargo, but no rights in the cargo. This position is variable only in a time of emergency, when the shipowner receives implied powers of agency to act, on behalf of the cargo owner, according to the circumstances.

Ballast. Weighty material carried to ensure stability of the ship. Present-day use of water as a ballasting material saves time and expense and is the most efficient medium for use.

Baltcon. Baltic and White Sea Conference Coal Charter Party 1921 for Scandinavia and White Sea.

Baltime. 1939 Baltic and White Sea Conference General Time Charter Party.

Baltimore Form C. Grain Charter Party form for East Coast North America to Continent.

Baltpulp. Baltic and International Maritime Conference Baltic Pulp and Paper Charter Party for Finland/U.K. Continent.

Bar Draft. (B.D.). The depth of water over a bar. Unless specified this should be the draft at the ebb tide. Authorities of ports or rivers which have bars, and which have seasonal or periodical draft variations, provide details of draft measurements for users of the area.

Bareboat Charter. Charterer hires ship and pays all expenses during the period of the hire.

Barratry. A fraudulent act on the part of the master and/or the crew of a vessel against the interest of the shipowner or cargo owner, without the connivance of the shipowner.

Barrel. Contains 36 gallons. The U.S.A. Barrel contains 42 gallons. Barrel of Butter 224 lb.

Base. Home depot of container.

Battens. Pieces of wood not more than 5 in. wide and less than 2 in. thick, and in length from 6 to 30 feet.

B.B. Certificate that the master has deposited log book and crew list with the shipping office of the mercantile marine.

B. Bridge. Notation of a deck erection in *Lloyd's Register*.

B.C. Bristol Channel. This expression usually covers the South Wales ports of Newport, Swansea, Port Talbot and Cardiff, in addition to Bristol, Avonmouth, Portishead and Sharpness.

B.D. See **Bar Draft.**

Bells. Used to denote ship's time. The bell is rung from midnight onwards at each half hour, increasing by one ring until eight bells is sounded. The ring then reverts to one bell, which again is increased half-hourly by an additional ring. Thus:—

0030 One bell	0200 Four bells	0330 Seven bells
0100 Two bells	0230 Five bells	0400 Eight bells
0130 Three bells	0300 Six bells	0430 One bell

Eight bells rings at 0400, 0800, 1200, 1600 and 2400 hours.

One bell is also rung 15 minutes before each watch—0345, 0745, etc.

The period from 1600 hrs. to 2000 hrs is divided into two Dog Watches—1600 hrs. to 1800 hrs., and 1800 hrs. to 2000 hrs. Dog Watches being half the time of a full watch ring only to four bells.

Benacon. Chamber of Shipping British North American (Atlantic) Wood Charter Party 1914.

Berth. The appointed place in a dock, at a quay or at a jetty where the vessel may load, discharge, or lay.

Berthage. The charge for use of a berth.

Berthing Note. A form of chartering contract used by ship-brokers who engage cargoes for ships, on a commission basis, but exclude liability of the broker for freight or demurrage.

Bill of Health. Certificate issued by the Medical Officer of Health for the port, giving a statement of the condition of health of the port or the ship.

Bill of Lading (B.L.). A receipt given by the carrier or his agent for goods received for shipment, or shipped on board a vessel. It is a quasi-negotiable document of title, and whilst not a contract, contains prima-facie evidence of the terms of such. See also **Set of Bills of Lading.**

Bill of Sale. Is the document used to transfer ownership in a British ship and requires registration. Such a bill has nothing to do with a bill of sale under the Bills of Sale Act, 1878.

Bill of Sight. Entry by an importer of goods the full details of which are not known. The Customs Authorities inspect the cargo, obtain details, and the importer then completes his entry. This completion is known as " Perfecting the Sight."

Bill of Store. Entry required for the re-importation of British goods within a stated period, which frees the goods from the conditions applicable to foreign goods.

B.L. See Bill of Lading.

Blockade. The prevention of the use of a port or country, usually attained by force, *e.g.* warships, mines, aircraft, etc.

Blue-peter. A blue flag with white rectangular centre and standing for letter " P " in the international code of signals. It is hoisted when a ship is about to sail.

Boards. Pieces of wood under 2 in. in thickness and more than 4 in. wide.

B.O.B. Barges on board. (Variant of LASH and Seabee but with a different concept of stowage and handling.)

Bollard. Post on a ship or quay to which are secured mooring ropes.

B.M.F. Board measurement feet. A basis of charging freight on cargoes of timber.

Bona fide. In good faith.

Bond. A promise or obligation, *e.g.* Bond for " free goods " is the shipper's promise to re-export; Average Bond, the promise to pay Average contributions when assessed.

Bonded Goods. Goods which are deposited in a bonded warehouse until such time as the duty upon them has been paid.

Bonded Warehouse. Warehouse where the owners have entered into a bond promising to pay duty when goods are removed for consumption.

B.o.T. Board of Trade (now Dept. of Trade and Industry).

Bottomry. Money borrowed upon a ship's hull, gear, and/ or cargo which is repayable with interest or premium when the vessel returns to port in safety. The loan is forfeited should the vessel sink, but the lender has an insurable interest in the ship whilst the payment is outstanding.

Bottomry Bond. The bond used when the vessel is pledged under bottomry.

Breaking Bulk (or Breaking Out). The opening up of a hold and the commencement of discharge.

Bridge Deck Ship. A vessel fitted with one deck above the shelter deck.

Britcont. General Home Trade Charter Party 1928.

British Ship. A ship which is owned wholly by persons entitled to own a British ship (see under **Shipowner**).

Broken Stowage. Space lost which is caused by the stowage of unevenly shaped packages.

Brokerage. Commission charged for securing and transacting business.

Brokers. (See **Ship Brokers**.) Specialized intermediaries.

Brought to and taken from alongside. Ship will accept cargo for loading only if it is brought to the ship's side. Discharge of cargo is also to be at ship's side. Responsibility in getting cargo to and from alongside is not the ship's.

B.S. Indication in *Lloyd's Register* of Classification under British Corporation, before amalgamation of the Societies.

B.S.T. British summer time.

b/t. Berth terms.

Builder's Certificate. Necessary document required in the registration of a ship, giving particulars of the ship, and details of the persons who are entitled to be registered as owners.

Bulcon. Chamber of shipping 1911 Bulgarian Berth Contract Grain Charter Party form.

Bulkhead. Partition dividing one part of a ship from another, not always watertight unless so specified, *e.g.* collision bulkhead.

Bumboat. A boat used for supplying provisions and stores to ships at a port of call.

Bunker. Space in which fuel for the vessel is stored on board. The expression " bunkers " denotes the fuel itself. Vessels which use oil for propulsion have fuel tanks instead of a bunker, often being located in the ship's double bottom and other parts of the ship which interfere as little as possible with the vessel's earning capacity.

Butt. A large cask containing 126 gallons.

C

C. Notation in *Lloyd's Register* that ship's engines are compound engines.

Cable. A measure of length. The length of a cable is 600 ft. or 100 fathoms.

Cancelling date. The date stated in the charter party at which the charterer may cancel the contract if the vessel has not given notice of readiness or equivalent.

C. and F. Cost and freight. A " C. and F." price includes not only the cost but also the freight.

C. and I. Price quoted includes cost of goods and insurances.

Captain's Entry. A provisional entry passed by the captain of a ship, when it is desirable to discharge the whole of the cargo at some particular place, or in cases where the merchant has omitted to pass the prime entry within the prescribed time.

Captain's Protest. A declaration made by the captain of a ship, giving details of damage, suspected damage or accident to his ship or cargo.

Cargo. Merchandise for carriage on board a ship.

Cargo Battens. Battens fitted into the ship for the purpose of keeping cargo away from immediate contact with the ship's side.

Cargo Book. A book kept by shipbrokers, containing the weight, mark, numbers, and measurement of all goods taken on board ship, and stating whether they were received by land or water.

Cargo carrying capacity. The capacity of the ship for cargo may be expressed in various ways, *e.g.* deadweight cargo capacity, measurement tons, or bill of lading or freight tons. Care should be taken to ascertain which figure is being quoted when referring to cargo capacity. In some trades, the ship's capacity may be referred to in trade units, *e.g.* standards, quarters, etc.

Carriage of Goods by Sea Act, 1924. See **C. of G. Act.**

Car Seal. Numbered seals (recorded in covering documents) used in conjunction with locking mechanism of containers.

Carving Note. The authority issued by H.M. Customs (after the ship has been registered) giving permission for the name of the vessel to be put on in the case of a new ship, or to alter the name in the case of a change of name. This term is a survival of the olden days when permission to " carve " the name on wooden ships was granted.

Casus Belli. An act which causes or justifies war.

Cattle Manifest. A document used by those vessels which carry cattle, and contains full particulars of the cattle shipped on board.

Causa Causans. The real or actual cause. In a succession of incidents which contribute to a loss or damage, the combined influence of all the incidents is considered as the real or actual cause.

Causa Proxima. The nearest cause; the immediate or final cause of accident or damage. *Causa proxima* arises only when a succession of incidents have contributed to the loss or damage.

Causa Remota. The furthest or first cause in a series of incidents which give rise to a loss.

Caveat Emptor. A legal expression meaning " let the buyer beware." A purchaser must, unless goods are sold by warranty or sample, in his own interests ascertain their state and condition before he makes a purchase.

C.B.H. (or Cont.B(H)). Continent Bordeaux/Hamburg Range of Ports.

C.C. Civil commotion.

C.D.V. Current domestic value of the goods in their country of origin. Used for calculating import duty.

Cellular Vessel. Ship specially constructed for stowage of containers in vertical stacks six high.

Cemenco. Chamber of Shipping 1923 Cement Charter Party form for sailing ships.

Centrocon. Chamber of Shipping River Plate/Homewards Charter Party 1914 form.

Certificate of Damage. This is a document, in printed form, issued by dock companies, when goods are received by them in a damaged condition as they are landed from a ship.

Certificate of Origin. A consular certificate sometimes required as a supporting document to a bill of lading; it gives full particulars of the country of origin of the goods.

Certificate of Ownership. Or Certificate of Registry; the ship's document of identity showing the details of ship and particulars of ownership.

Certificate of Registry. Commonly known as the " ship's register," this contains, *inter alia*, details of the ship and its registered number. It has no value as a document of title to the ship, but is only a registration document. Sect. 15 of the Merchant Shipping Act, 1894, provides that it shall not be subject to detention by reason of any title, lien, charge or interest claimed by any owner, mortgagor or other person.

Cesser Clause. The clause in a charter party which provides that the charterer's obligations under the contract (namely the loading of the cargo and the payment of charges) being fulfilled, his liability ceases. As this clause is usually joined with the shipowner's lien clause, it creates the position that a charge subsequently raised may automatically revive the charterer's liability, which ceased at an earlier date.

C.F.I. See **C.I.F.**

C.F.O. Calling for orders. These letters added to documents and followed by a named port or place, give the vessel the right to break her voyage and collect orders for discharging port. This occurs when a vessel is fixed " UK/Continent " and leaves her final port before actual discharging ports are nominated.

C.F.S. Container Freight Station operated by a carrier for assembling or distributing the shipments into or out of his containers.

c.ft. Cubic foot. The volume of a cube whose edge is equal to one foot. The basis of a freight ton is 40 cu. ft., and a ship's ton is 100 cu. ft.

c.g.a. Cargo's proportion of general average, which is based upon the arrived value of the cargo at destination.

Chaldron (of coal). 25½ Imperial cwt. 53 Cwt., Newcastle.

Charges Forward. A term used in accounts when the carriage and other charges are to be paid by the buyer upon receipt of the goods.

Charterer. One who hires a vessel for a voyage or period of time.

Chartering Broker. The shipbroker who acts as an intermediary between the owner of the ship and the charterer, in regard to rates of freight, and terms of the contract.

Charter Party. Contract between a shipowner and charterer for the carriage of goods on a stated voyage (voyage charter party), or for a period of time (time charter party). Time charter parties may, under certain conditions, be described as demise charter parties (q.v.).

Charter Party deletions. When a clause is deleted from a charter party, the clause is ignored in every respect and the charter party is to be read as if the clause never appeared in the document. For example, if a clause which provides that the steamer shall have the option of discharging at Hamburg is deleted, the document is not to be read to the effect that " as option of discharging at Hamburg has been deleted, the ship now has no such option."

Check weighing or check measuring. The operation of instituting a second check upon details when a dispute has occurred. It is usual for the person requesting the check to pay the expenses if the original information supplied is found

23

to be correct. If wrong, the supplier of the original information meets the charge.

C.H.H. (or Cont. H/H). Continent Havre/Hamburg Range of Ports.

C.I.B. Corporation of Insurance Brokers.

C.I.E. Captain's imperfect entry.

C.I.F. Cost, insurance and freight. A price " C.I.F." means that it includes the cost of goods, their insurance, and freight. Whilst the purchaser of c.i.f. goods bears no expenses until he takes the goods from the ship at destination, due fulfilment by the seller may take place when he passes to the buyer the invoice, insurance policy, and bill of lading.

C.I.F.C.I. Term of sale which includes cost, insurance, freight, commission and interest.

C.I.F.E. Cost, insurance, freight and exchange; the price of goods includes insurance, freight and costs of foreign exchange.

C.I.F.LT. Cost, insurance and freight, London terms. (See also **L.C.**—London Clause.)

C.I.I. Chartered Insurance Institute (Fellow, F.C.I.I.; Associate, A.C.I.I.).

C.I.M. Comite Maritime International.

C.L. Indication in *Lloyd's Register* that propellor shaft is fitted with a continuous liner.
Also, Container Load. A shipment sufficient to fill a container.

Classification. Comparison with an ideal; grading according to quality.

Clean. In shipping parlance, bills of lading, mate's receipts, and such like documents are said to be " *clean* " when no clauses detrimental to the shippers have been inserted in them, and " *dirty*," " *unclean*," or " *foul*," when they state that the goods were not shipped in good order and condition.

Clearance. Official permission from the appropriate authority for a vessel to leave port when all dues have been paid and all formalities observed.

Clearance Terminal. Container terminal with customs facilities where dutiable goods may enter country.

Clear Days. The calculation of time which is reckoned as complete, or unbroken days.

Closed Indent. An order to a supplier for goods of a named or specified manufacture. Such an order gives the buyer no opportunity to take advantage of competitive offers.

Closing date. The final date up to which the vessel is available to accept cargo for shipment. This may vary according to the trade from two or three days. It is to allow for the preparation of documents by the time the ship sails.

c.m. Cubic metre—35.3148 cu. ft.

C.N.C. Compagnie Nationale des Containers.

Coastcon. Chamber of Shipping Coasting Coal Charter Party form 1920.

Coastcon Sailer. Chamber of Shipping 1923 Coasting Charter Party for Sailing vessels, England and Scotland— United Kingdom and the Continent.

Coasters. Vessels employed in the coasting trade between home ports only; so-called because they do not sail far from land, but keep somewhat close to the sea-shore.

Coasting Trade. The coasting trade of any country refers to the commerce carried on by ships which do not go abroad, but trade between home ports only.

C.O.D. Cash on delivery.

Cofferdam. A double watertight bulkhead usually found in tankers, dividing the oil tanks from the engines of the vessel.

C. of G. Act. Carriage of Goods by Sea Act, 1924. An Act to regulate the relationship between the shipper and ship-owner in contracts of affreightment governed by bills of lading.

Common Carrier. Any carrier who by the nature of his service provides a conveyance for goods and must, with certain exceptions, accept any goods offered for carriage. He is liable for the goods whilst they are in his care and may claim exception only for loss arising by Act of God, Queen's enemies, and inherent vice. Fire, negligence of shipper and general average, can be included as these are common law rights available to all carriers, whether common carriers or not.

A shipowner contends that for the safety of the adventure he must preserve the right to refuse any unsuitable cargo, that all his freight contracts are made by special agreement, and he is therefore not a common carrier. The fact that the Carriage of Goods by Sea Act, 1924, provides a list of exemptions, and the Merchant Shipping Act, 1894, allows a limitation of liability, must indicate that the shipowner is not confined to the common carrier's obligations.

Common Law Lien. The rights of a person, provided for by common law, to hold goods until charges incurred by such goods have been paid. (See **Possessory Lien** and **Compulsory Sale.**)

Complement. The total number of persons which constitutes a full crew employed on a ship.

Compulsory Sale. The sale of goods or property which takes place after the exercise of a lien and the non-payment of charges. The lien holder must retain the goods for a period of 90 days (excluding perishable goods which have an immediate sale), during which time tender of payment of charges and accrued warehouse expenses frees the goods from the lien. After 90 days the holder must advertise the sale in prescribed newspapers or publications and hold a public sale. The money received is then disposed of by the payment of customs and excise fees; expenses of the sale; payment of warehouse fees and expenses; landing charges, and settlement of the lien. Any balance left belongs to the late owner of the cargo and must be held for his account.

Concurrent with discharge. Where payment of freight is specified in this manner, freight is to be paid proportionately to the quantity discharged from time to time at intervals throughout the operation. The shipowner will have the right of holding up delivery if the freight is not paid up to date.

Conference Lines. An association of the shipowning lines which operates in a given trade, whereby standard or tariff rates are fixed and a regular service operated for the mutual benefit of both the merchant trading in that area and the shipowner who runs his line. Against the disadvantage of being a "semi-monopoly," (although no shipping company can ever be described as a monopoly in the true sense), the shipper gains by non-competitive soundly operated services which are available during the year, and remain constant irrespective of boom or slump.

Congenbill. Chamber of Shipping Bill of Lading for timber cargoes from Germany to U.K.

Consign. To send goods from one place to another.

Consignee. The person to whom the goods are sent. He has the same powers of suit against the shipowner as the owner of the goods (Bill of Lading Act, 1885).

Consignment. The act of consigning, or the goods themselves. In shipping, this expression is invariably used to denote the goods, *e.g.* an order for 100 boilers may be despatched in ten consignments of ten boilers. The act of consigning is usually referred to as " sending forward."

Consignment Notes. Forms used by some shipping companies as receiving and forwarding notes, when goods are received by them and shipped without bills of lading being issued.

Consignor. The person who consigns or sends the goods forward.

Consolidate. When more than one shipment for different consignees is combined in a container.

Constructive Total Loss. See C.T.L.

Consul. The commercial representative of one nation, residing officially in another country, whose duties are mainly to facilitate business relations between the two countries.

Consulage. Fees paid to a consul for the protection of goods, for signing documents, and for other services rendered.

Consular Invoice. An invoice, legalized by a consul, giving details of the goods which enable foreign Customs duties to be correctly charged.

Cont. B/H. Continent range of ports between Bordeaux and Hamburg.

Cont. H/H. Continent Havre/Hamburg range.

Contcoal. Baltic and International Maritime Conference Charter Party 1945 for coal and coke from Germany, Netherlands and Belgium.

Contingency Freight. The insurable interest which is created by the assured paying freight on arrival.

Continuation Clause. Applicable to marine insurance policies effected for a period of time. Should the interest (object of insurance) be at sea at the expiry of the policy, this clause grants an extension of the insurance until the interest reaches port. An additional premium (q.v.) is payable for this extension.

Contraband. Goods smuggled into a country, avoiding payment of Customs duty, or forbidden goods.

Contract of Affreightment. See **Affreightment.**

Contwood. Baltic and International Maritime Conference Charter Party 1937 for wood from Baltic (ex USSR) and Norway to Continent.

Cord. A cord of wood measures 4 ft. by 4 ft. by 8 ft. or 128 cu. ft.

C. ore 7. Ore Charter Party for use in Mediterranean.

C. ore 8. Ore Charter Party from Bay of Biscay.

Cost and Freight. See **C. and F.**

Cost, Insurance and Freight. See **C.I.F.**

C/P. Charter party (q.v.).

c.p.d. Charterer pays dues. Any dues incurred in the course of fulfilment of the charter party are for account of the charterer and not the shipowner.

C.R. Current rate (Stevedoring cost).

Craft. In marine insurance, the word " craft " means any barge, lighter, river trader, or any other boat or vessel employed in carrying, shipping, or discharging the goods insured.

Cranage. A charge made at some ports for the hire of a crane when used for loading or unloading such goods from a ship (which are too heavy for the ordinary tackle on board).

Credits. There are three main types of credit:—
(1) The confirmed irrevocable credit, which is an irrevocable undertaking given by an overseas bank and confirmed by a British bank, to pay the seller, provided certain documents are tendered within a certain time. Furthermore, not only is the undertaking irrevocable on the part of the foreign bank but the confirmation given by the United Kingdom bank is also irrevocable.

(2) The irrevocable credit, which carries the irrevocable undertaking only of the foreign bank, whose British correspondent merely advises the terms of the credit without assuming any liability to the beneficiary.

(3) The unconfirmed, or, as it is sometimes called, the revocable credit. As its name implies this credit may be cancelled at any time, with or without notice to the beneficiary. It does not incorporate any irrevocable undertaking to pay on the part of either the foreign bank or its British correspondent, and consequently its use is limited.

Crew Agreement. The agreement in writing between the seaman employed, and the person employing him in accordance with Board of Trade regulations.

Crew List. The list of crew, and capacity in which each serves, which document is part of the " ship's papers." Sometimes this list is known as the " Muster Roll."

C.T. Container Terminal where large scale handling and storage facilities are available for two or more forms of transportation.

C.T.C. Corn Trade Clauses.

C.T.L. Constructive total loss. This occurs when goods or ship are involved in peril, and are placed in such a position that the cost of recovery and making good would exceed the value of the property itself.

C.T.L.O. Constructive total loss only.

Cube Out. When the measurement capacity of the container has been reached before the weight limit.

Custom of Trade. A permissible plea which allows for a trade custom to be included in the reading of the contract. A custom of trade must be a procedure which has been in operation so long in the trade or area that it is recognized by all involved as the customary mode of operation. In such case a custom of trade may be read into the terms of the contract, and will over-ride methods to the contrary which are stipulated. Where, however, terms which are not in conformity with custom are added to the document with a proviso " in spite of custom " then such conditions will apply.

Customs Bills of Entry are daily lists issued by the Customs authorities (to merchants and others subscribing), containing a summary of British shipping, useful for general information.

Customs Duties. The duties payable to Customs authorities.

Customs Entry. A list given to the Customs authorities by the importer or shipper, showing the weight, value, and description of goods to be landed or shipped. See **Entry.**

Customs Preventive Officer. A Customs officer—commonly known as the Rummaging Officer—whose duty it is to prevent smuggling or the introduction into the country of any goods other than by the normal legal channels.

D

D/A (or D.A.A.). Documents against Acceptance. Documents are transferred against the acceptance of the Bill of Exchange.

Dancon. Chamber of Shipping Grain Charter Party 1911 for Danube berth contracts.

Danger Money. Extra payment made to those engaged in work which entails more than the usual risk of personal injury.

D.B.B. Deals, boards and battens. See separate entries for measurements.

Dbk. Drawback (q.v.).

D.B.S. Distressed British seaman. A British seaman who is left abroad by reason of sickness, accident, termination of agreement, loss of ship, desertion, etc., where the liability remains for his employer to pay the cost of his return home to his proper return port.

D.C. Deviation clause. A clause in a bill of lading or charter party giving the ship rights to deviate during the contract. This clause is reliable only in the event of a justifiable deviation. A deviation clause in marine insurance contracts gives the assured the right to have the policy extended to cover the deviation upon payment of a suitable additional premium (q.v.).

dd. (or deld.). Delivered.

Deadfreight. Freight paid for space booked but not used. This is calculated at full freight on cargo which should have been loaded, less the amount of charges, *e.g.* handling, loading costs, etc., which would have been incurred had cargo been shipped. Whilst the shipowner has the right to enforce deadfreight on all shipments, it is usually applied only to charter party contracts.

Deals. Pieces of wood measuring 7–9 in. wide, 2 in. or more thick, and between 6 ft. and 30 ft. in length.

2—(B.437/B.1040)

Debenture. A certificate given by the Custom House to the exporter of excisable goods, entitling him to receive payment of the drawback allowed on such goods being exported.

Deck Cargo or **Deck Load.** Cargo which is carried on deck. All deck cargo is governed by Board of Trade regulations, and by special arrangement with the shipper. Carriage on deck does not, normally, constitute " stowage " in its correct meaning. Deck cargo is outside the terms of the Carriage of Goods by Sea Act, 1924.

Deck Cargo Certificate. Certificate given by Customs Officer of the quantity of deck cargo carried by vessel.

Declaration of Ownership. The declaration which a person must give to be entitled to own a British ship. It contains details of his qualification to own, details of where the ship was built, name of master, number of shares to be registered, and a statement that no unauthorized person is entitled to a beneficial interest in the ship.

Del credere. An agreement by which an agent, when he sells goods on credit guarantees, for an additional commission, the solvency of the buyer and his performance of the contract.

Delegation. The power of an agent to entrust the performance of his own duties to another person. Delegation may take place only with the agreement of the principal.

Deletion of Charter Party Clauses. See **Charter Party deletions.**

Delivery Order. An order from the owner of goods lying at a warehouse, dock, or wharf, requesting the superintendent to deliver either the whole, or a portion of the goods, to the bearer of the order, or the party named thereon by endorsement. Delivery orders are also issued by shipowners to consignees in exchange for bills of lading at port of discharge.

Demise Charter Party. A time charter party in which the terms of the contract amount to a virtual change of ownership during the period of hire. The charterer provides not only his own crew, but also his own Master and Chief Engineer.

Demurrage. Compensation paid to the shipowner for delay of a vessel beyond the stipulated time allowed in the charter party for loading or discharge. The usual manner of calculating demurrage is at an agreed rate per net registered ton per day.

Deposit Receipt. The receipt given for the payment of a general average deposit. Such a deposit is a payment on account of the full proportion of general average which will be ascertained at a later date when the average adjuster has completed settlement.

Depreciation. Loss of value by obsolescence, wear and tear, changed circumstances, etc. The act of reducing the value of a vessel to keep this at or below its market value, or preferably cost price. Writing down values depends upon the finances of the company and its trading results.

Despatch Half Demurrage ($D\frac{1}{2}D$). The rate of despatch money is half the rate charged for demurrage.

$D\frac{1}{2}D$ A.T.S.B.E. Despatch half demurrage on all time saved both ends.

$D\frac{1}{2}D$ W.T.S.B.E. Despatch half demurrage on working time saved both ends.

Devanning. Unloading the contents from a container.

Deviation. Departure from the set or agreed course of the voyage. The action may be justifiable, *e.g.* in the interests of all parties to the adventure, or unjustifiable when the deviation is against the interest of one or more parties to the adventure. If deviation is unlawful, the underwriter comes off risk from the moment of deviation, and the shipowner thereupon becomes, in effect, the insurer of the cargo for the remainder of the voyage. Deviation may arise through delay.

D.f. Notation in *Lloyd's Register* that ship is fitted with Direction Finding apparatus.

Dirty Bill of Lading. See **Unclean Bill of Lading.**

Dirty Money. Extra payment made to labourers for handling goods of an objectionable nature.

Disbursements. Money expended for the purpose of ship's expenses. This includes wages, stores, fuel, loading and discharging expenses.

Discharge Book. The identity book and records of service of a seaman. It contains a description of the holder and details of previous employment—name of ship, capacity in which he served, and conduct report.

Dispatch Money. Payment, by way of a bonus, to the charterer for loading or discharging a vessel in less time than is stipulated in the charter party. Generally based upon a set figure per day or *pro-rata*, or " dispatch half demurrage."

Displacement. The actual weight in tons of 2,240 lb. of the ship. A term applied to naval craft but rarely used in connection with merchant ships.

Disseminate. To unload and divide the contents of a container into separate deliveries.

Dock and Town Dues. Dock and Town Dues are peculiar to the port of Liverpool. They are chargeable on most goods exported from, or imported into that city, the town dues being levied, it seems, for the use of the *port*, whether a vessel carries goods into the dock or not.

Dock Dues. Charges made upon shipping for the use of the docks. These are calculated on registered tonnage and deck load, if any.

Dock Warrant. A receipt given for goods deposited in a dock warehouse.

Dock Weight Note. See **Weight Note.**

Documentary Bill. A bill of lading with bill of exchange, invoice, insurance policy and sometimes a letter of hypothecation in support.

D.P. Days purposes.

D/P. Documents against Payment. Documents are transferred against payment of charges.

d.p. Direct port. Vessel proceeds to the named port without making intermediate calls.

Draftage. Allowance off freight on grain cargoes where grain is discharged and weighed by approved hopper scale in drafts of 2,000 lbs or over.

Draught. Depth of water. The draught of a ship is the depth of water which is necessary to float her. Care should be taken to differentiate between light draught (of the unladen ship) and the loaded draught.

Drawback. The allowance granted by Customs authorities. It is a return, on re-exportation, of duty paid at time of importation.

Dry Dock. Is used for the examination and repair of ships, which are admitted at high water, and left dry by the ebbing of the tide before the gates are closed; or the gates are closed as soon as the ships are admitted, the water being let out by pulling up the sluices, or pumped out.

Dumb barge. A barge without sail or motive power.

Dunnage. Material used by the ship in the stowage of cargo for packing, separation of cargo, or in other ways to prevent damage to cargo whilst on the voyage.

Dutiable Stores. Stores which, if disposed of whilst the vessel is in port, would be dutiable. Upon arrival of the ship a list of dutiable stores is prepared, and these are locked and sealed by the Customs Preventive Officer against the ship's stay in port. Such stores are known as surplus stores, and a return of these must be lodged with the Customs House.

d.w. Deadweight, measured in tons of 2,240 lb. Deadweight cargo capacity is the weight (in tons) of the cargo required to sink the ship to her loadline after allowing for bunkers, stores, etc.

D.w.a.t. Deadweight all told.

D.w.c.c. Deadweight cargo capacity.

E

E. and O.E. Errors and omissions excepted.

E.C.C.P. East Coast (United Kingdom) Coal Port.

E.C.G.B. East Coast Great Britain.

E.C.U.K. East Coast United Kingdom.

Ejusdem generis. The doctrine of *ejusdem generis* applies to general expressions added to a list of phrases. Where the clause " pirates, rovers, thieves, or any other cause " appears, the words " or any other cause " may by this doctrine apply only to any other cause similar to pirates, rovers or thieves. But where the general words appear first, *e.g.* " any cause, pirates, rovers, thieves, etc." the general words are not governed by the specified items—these are mere examples.

Embargo. A Government prohibition against the movement of ships or cargoes in certain areas.

Endorsement of Bill. If the bill of lading is made out to a named consignee, that person must endorse the bill before he can obtain delivery of his cargo. Should the bill be consigned to " Order " or " shipper's Order " the shipper must endorse the bill before he parts with it. The rules of endorsement, as applicable to cheques and other documents, apply equally to bills of lading. Under the Bills of Lading Act, 1855, the endorser taking delivery and endorsement by way of absolute transfer has all the rights and duties of the original shipper under the contract evidenced by the bill of lading.

Entrepot. An intermediate port or warehouse for use by goods which are in transit.

Entry. To pass Customs entry is to give the authorities an exact description of goods to be shipped or landed, and pay the duty (if any) upon them. Goods arriving are " entered inwards," and those shipped, " entered outwards."

Entry for Free Goods. The Customs form required giving details of cargo imported which is free of import duty.

Entry for Warehousing. A Custom House document issued when dutiable goods are imported, but are to be stored in a Government or bonded warehouse until required for use.

E.s.d. Indication in *Lloyd's Register* that vessel is fitted with Echo Sounding Device.

Ex. Out of.

Excise. Duty charged on home produced goods before sale to the consumer.

Ex facie. According to documents.

Ex gratia. Act of grace.

Exports. Goods shipped out of a country, and sold abroad. **Invisible Exports,** the services which bring money into the country, *e.g.* Shipping services, or Insurances, although intangible are sold abroad in the same way as Exports.

Express Authority. An authority given expressly by writing or word of mouth.

Ex quay. Purchaser is responsible for charges after delivery on quay.

Ex ship. Seller pays freight to port of destination. All other charges are for account of the purchaser. The ship must be at place where it is usual for the goods to be delivered (*Yangtze Ins. Assn.* v. *Lukmanjee,* [1918] A.C. 585). The term " Free Overside " has the same meaning.

Extended Protest. This occurs when the shipmaster makes a detailed protest of an event when this information is required for subsequent legal action. Besides making the protest under oath the master and mate must sign the statement.

Ex Warehouse. Cost " ex warehouse " means that the buyer pays all charges for insurance, freight, etc.

F

F. Forecastle (q.v.). The abbreviation is used in *Lloyd's Register*. The abbreviation also indicates the freshwater marking of the loadline grid.

F.A.A. Free of all average.

F.A. or F.A.S. Free alongside or free alongside ship. Terms of purchase provide for the supply of goods alongside the vessel at seller's expense and risk. Any costs of handling the cargo and loading are then for account of the purchaser. The seller must give the buyer sufficient notice to enable him to insure the goods during the sea voyage. (Sale of Goods Act, 1894, Sect. 32(3).)

f.a.c. Fast as can. Expression in documents to the effect that ship shall load (or discharge) as fast as she can take on board (or deliver). There is implied an obligation upon the part of the charterer to supply the cargo as fast as the ship requires it. The term should not be read as an obligation to take cargo at a rate which is in excess of the customary daily discharging rate of the port. See also **As fast as can.**

Faggot (of steel). 120 lbs.

F.A.S. See **F.A.**

Fatal Accidents Act, 1846. See **Lord Campbell's Act.**

Fathom. A measure of length. A nautical fathom is equal to six feet. A fathom of timber is a stack of wood measuring 6 ft. by 6 ft. by 6 ft. = 216 cu. ft.

f.c. & s. Free of capture and seizure. The insured excludes losses arising from capture or seizure whilst the goods are insured.

F.C.L. Full Container Load. When the load reaches its maximum weight or measurement permitted.

F.C.R. Forwarders Certificate of Receipt. The Forwarding Agents own document for through goods.

F.D. Free despatch.

f.d. Free delivery. Charges for delivery are not for account of the purchaser.

f. & d. Freight and demurrage. The charge is inclusive of freight and any demurrage which may be incurred.

Ferticon. Chamber of Shipping 1942 Fertiliser Charter.

F.G.A. Free of general average. Underwriter does not cover claims for cargo owner's proportion of general average contributions. See also **Foreign General Average.**

f.i.a. Full interest admitted. Underwriter has accepted the assured's interest in the subject matter of the insurance, and will not subsequently dispute this.

f.i.b. Free into bunkers or free into barge. Price quoted includes cost of loading into bunkers (or barge).

f.i.o. Free in and out. The rate quoted is exclusive to ship-owners of cost of loading and discharge. These are borne by shipper or charterer.

f.i.o.s. Free in and out and st owed.

f.i.o.t.   Free in and out of trucks.

Fire.   An excepted peril which all carriers exclude unless fire is caused by the privity of the shipowner or carrier.

Firewood.   Ends of timber measuring under 6 ft.

f.i.w.   Free into wagons.   Seller pays all expenses up to and including loading costs into wagons or trucks, but the rail charges are for account of purchaser.

Flo Con.   Floating Containers.

Floating Policy.   A policy for a certain amount insuring goods which are not all in one place, but are spread over a certain district or area, so that the goods, wherever they may be deposited, are covered, either wholly or in part, according as their aggregate value may happen to be either under or above the sum insured.   This policy may also cover a series of shipments, the value of each being declared until the amount of the policy is exhausted.

Flotsam.   Goods lost by shipwreck or cast overboard which remain afloat.   If unclaimed within a year and a day they belong to the Crown.

f.o.b.   Free on board.   The vendor sells the goods at a price which includes all charges which are incurred in placing the goods on board the vessel.   Once the goods are on board the buyer bears the risk and subsequent expenses (*Melis and Stock*; 1885).   Delivery is complete once the goods have been put aboard ship.   Custom of port frequently varies the type of expense and service which falls for account of the seller.

f.o.c.   Free of charge.   Cost is inclusive of all expenses.

f.o.d.   Free of damage.

43

f.o.q. Free on quay. Price includes supply to wharf or quay, but does not include expenses of loading the cargo on board.

f.o.r. Free on rail. As **f.i.w.** or **f.o.t.**

Forecastle. The forecastle is situated at the forward end of the ship. Abbreviation F., used in *Lloyd's Register*.

Foreign General Average. Used in marine insurance, this term implies that general average will be paid by the underwriters, in accordance with an average statement made abroad.

Foreign Trade. The trade transacted with a country abroad.

Form A. American charter party for the cotton trade.

Forwarder's Bill of Lading. The bill of lading issued by the on-carrying company to the original shipping company when goods are sent forward on a voyage completed by two steamers. Also the bill issued by a shipping agent for a consignment covering composite voyages.

Forward SH./E. or Forward SHEX. See S/H.E.

f.o.t. Free on truck. See **f.i.w.**

Foul Bill of Lading. See **Unclean Bill of Lading.**

Founder. To fill with water and sink.

f.o.w. First open water. Instead of a stated date of readiness in the charter party, the term f.o.w. may be used to apply to ports which are ice-bound during winter months. It is the obligation of the shipowner to present his vessel at the first opportunity of the ship to enter the port free from ice obstructions.

F.P. See **Floating policy.**

f.p.a. Free of particular average. An exceptive clause which excludes particular average losses.

Franco. Prepaid or free of all charges. Price includes all charges up to and including delivery to buyer.

f.r.c.c. Free of riots and civil commotions. No liability arises for loss caused through riots or civil commotions.

Free Alongside. See **F.A.**

Freeboard. The distance between the waterline and the underside of the main deck of a ship, measured amidship.

Free of capture and seizure. See **f.c. & s.**

Free of encumbrances. An expression to be found in a bill of sale for ships, which indicates that there is no mortgage outstanding on the vessel. If a purchaser buys a ship, he also buys with it any maritime lien which can be attached to the vessel. Where a bill of sale is used in the purchase or transfer of a ship any such encumbrance must be declared in the document.

Free on board (quay, rail, etc.). See **f.o.b., f.o.r.,** etc.

Free Overside. See **Ex Ship.**

Free Turn. Ship is chartered or contracted for on the basis that she will be " free of turn," and not have to wait for a loading/discharging berth.

Freight. The sum paid for the hire of a ship, or a charge for carrying goods by water. See also **frt.** The term freight is sometimes loosely applied to cargo. This is confusing and should be avoided.

Freighter is a word often used for the charterer of a vessel, or by Americans as a description of a cargo ship.

Freight Collect or **Freight Forward.** Freight payable by consignee on arrival of the goods.

Freight Notes. Statements sent out by shipbrokers to the various shippers of goods showing the amount due for freight upon goods which have been taken on board ship.

Freight Release. An official document given by shipbrokers, or an endorsement by them on the bill of lading, authorizing the officer in charge of the ship to give up possession of the goods, the freight upon them having been paid.

Freight ton. A ton of cargo which is calculated upon the basis of 40 cu. ft. measurement, or 2,240 lb. weight. The ship has, unless otherwise provided by tariff rates, the option of charging freight on the basis which would show the greatest return. Goods weighing 10 cwt. but measuring 40 cu. ft. would be charged at measurement whilst goods weighing 40 cwt. and measuring 60 cu. ft. would be chargeable at weight rate.

frt. Freight. The consideration paid to the shipowner for the safe carriage and delivery of goods in a merchantable condition. Where the contract specifies freight as advance freight, lumpsum freight, etc., special conditions apply to the payment.

Frustration. The contract may be frustrated when circumstances arise which prevent the agreement from being carried out. Delay is a common cause of frustration. The expression is akin in many ways to the expression " impossible to perform." (q.v.).

F.S.F. Fellow of the Institute of Shipping and Forwarding Agents. Associate—A.S.F.

f.t. "Free turn" or "full terms" or "freight ton" (q.v.).

Full Terms. Chartering rate includes all commissions deductions, etc., as recognized in the particular trade in which ship is being operated.

F.W.C. Fully loaded weight and capacity. A container stowed to its maximum (weight or measurement).

G

G.A. General average. The law which provides the application of the principle of " that which is sacrificed for all is borne in proportion by all interested in the adventure."

G.A. Act. A term used to describe any extraordinary sacrifice or expenditure which has been intentionally and reasonably made or incurred for the common safety or for the purpose of preserving from peril the property involved in a common or maritime adventure.

Gallon. Imperial, 277.463 cu. in.; U.S.A., 231 cu. in.

Gc. Notation in *Lloyd's Register* that vessel is fitted with Gyro Compass.

Gencon. Baltic and White Sea Conference Uniform General Charter Party for all types of cargo with no particular trade.

General Average. See G.A.

General Average Account. The account which is opened to receive the payments made by contributors of their proportion of general average.

General Lien. A lien in which the right of holding property against the settlement of a charge raised on particular goods, is extended by the terms of the contract to any goods belonging to the same owner. The terms of a general lien may be extended from a shipment by one vessel to other shipments on other vessels.

Genorecon. Baltic and International Maritime Conference Charter Party 1962 for ore cargoes all over the world.

Germancon North. Baltic and International Maritime Conference Charter Party 1957 for coal, coke, and patent fuel from Ruhr District to Denmark, Finland, Norway and Sweden.

" Good " Ship. The warranty given by a shipowner in a charter party or on bills of lading outside the Carriage of Goods by Sea Act, 1924, that his vessel is seaworthy, and capable of withstanding the anticipated perils of the voyage.

Gothenburg Standard. Standard of pit props and sleepers measuring 180 cu. ft.

Grain Cargo Certificate. Certificate that grain cargo has been loaded in accordance with Board of Trade regulations. This applies only to grain cargoes from Mediterranean, Black Sea, or North American coast. The form is endorsed by Consular or Customs authority at final loading port.

Graving Dock. A dry dock.

Gross for Nett. When the difference in weight is so slight that it can be ignored, e.g. Bundles of tubes where wire binding is negligible, or bags of cement where weight of bags is ignored.

Gross Tonnage. Vessel's internal space measured in units of 100 cu. ft. Whilst no set figure can be given, a rough proportion of gross to net tonnage is $2\frac{1}{2}$:1.

Groundage. Charge made for permission to anchor.

Groupage. The service of providing facilities for the consolidation of small shipments into a container.

H

H.A.D. Havre, Antwerp or Dunkirk.

Hague Rules. Set of rules adopted at the International Maritime Law Conference held at Brussels in October, 1922, which formed the basis of legislation regulating the carriage of goods by sea in the ensuing years.

Harbour. A haven in which ships may anchor or moor. A harbour is only partly enclosed, and is so distinguished from a dock, which is wholly enclosed.

Harbour dues. Charges made upon a ship by the harbour authorities for use of the harbour.

Harter Act. American Act of Congress of 1893, relative to the carriage of goods by sea from or to American ports.

Hatchway. The name given to the opening in the decks of a ship giving access to the hold.

Haulage. Is an exclusive charge made by Railway, Dock, and Canal Companies for the use of carriages or trucks, the use of a line of rails, or the haulage of loaded or empty trucks or waggons between respective points. It does not cover the services of loading and discharging the trucks.

H.C. Held covered. The term used to denote that the insurance has been accepted by the insurer but no policy is in force. This contract is of no legal effect. The term is also incorporated into some policies and then means that should the risk not be exactly as insured the insurer will amend the policy on payment of an appropriate additional premium to cover the amended risk.

Heavy Grain. Consists of wheat, maize or rye. Where a grain charter allows other cargo to be shipped, the expression sometimes appears that this is permissible, such cargo paying the same rate as " heavy grain," *i.e.* the rate fixed by the charter for these commodities.

Held Covered. See H.C.

H.H.D.W. Heavy Handy Deadweight (Scrap).

High Seas. Unenclosed waters which are outside the boundaries of low water marks. Outside territorial waters the seas are free to all.

Hogged. When the two ends of the ship droop lower than the part amidships.

Hogshead. (abbr. Hhd.). A measure of capacity containing 54 gallons, or a large barrel containing this quantity.

Hold. A part of the interior of a vessel below deck in which cargo may be stowed.

Home Port. A port in the country of registration of ship, or nationality of seaman, *e.g.* a ship's home port is her registered port or her terminal port; and a seaman's home port is the port at which he signed on, or the port in his own country at which he signs off.

Home Trade. Trade carried on within the limits of the British Isles, and Elbe/Brest range of ports.

Home Use Entry. A Custom House document used when dutiable goods are to be removed from a warehouse for home consumption.

Hydrocharter. Charter party for Nitrate from Norway.

I

I.B. In bond. Goods are placed in a Customs bonded warehouse where they are retained without payment of Customs duties. Such goods are known as being " In bond." A useful method whereby the merchant pays duty only as he releases his cargo to purchasers, and invaluable when dealing with high duty goods such as tobacco, etc.

I.C.D. Inland Clearance Depot. Freight terminal away from the transportation terminal, where Customs facilities are available.

I.C.H.C.A. International Cargo Handling Co-ordination Association.

I.C.S. Institute of Chartered Shipbrokers; F.I.C.S. (Fellow), A.I.C.S. (Associate).

Implied authority. Where authority has been granted by implication and the agent is led to believe, or tacitly given to understand that the principal wishes him to act on his behalf.

Import List. An alphabetical list of headings under which imported goods are classified by the customs for statistical purposes.

Imports. A collective term for all goods and commodities brought into the country from some other nation or place.

Impossible to perform. Impossibility to perform may be successfully pleaded for the cancellation of a contract when some happening makes the fulfilment impossible. A change of law which prohibits the entry of an agreed cargo into a country is a good example.

Imposts are taxes, particularly those on imports.

In Ballast. When a vessel leaves a port without a cargo she is said to be in ballast, as she carries some kind of weight—water, gravel, sand, etc., to give her stability.

In Bond. See **I.B.**

Indemnity. Security against or compensation for loss or damage.

Indent. See **Open Indent.**

Indorsement of Bill. See **Endorsement of Bill.**

Inherent Vice. A defect due to the nature of the object, for example, disease of apples, "sleepiness" of pears, where the defect ultimately destroys the goods.

In Personam. An action against a particular individual, whereby a successful claimant has a right against the estate of the individual.

In Rem. An action against the thing itself (*e.g.* ship) whereby a successful claimant may attach his right, by way of a lien or arrest on the object, and obtain immediately some tangible security.

INST. T. Institute of Transport; M. INST. T. (Member), A. M. INST. T. (Associate).

In Transitu. On the passage. See also under **Stoppage in transitu.**

Invoice. A written account of particulars of goods delivered to a purchaser and of their price and the charges concerning them. An invoice is sufficient memorandum in writing of the contract within Sect. 4 of the Sale of Goods Act, 1893.

Inward Charges. The costs incurred upon a vessel entering port.

I.S.O. International Organization for Standardization.

I.T.A. Institute of Traffic Administration; **M.I.T.A.** (Member.)

J

Jason Clause. In the event of accident, danger, damage or disaster before or after the commencement of the voyage, resulting from any cause whatsoever, whether due to negligence or not, for which or for the consequence of which, the carrier is not responsible, by statute, contract or otherwise, the goods, shippers, consignees or owners of the goods shall contribute with the carrier in general average to the payment of any sacrifices, losses or expenses of a general average nature that may be made or incurred, and shall pay salvage and special charges incurred in respect of the goods.

If a salving ship is owned or operated by the carrier, salvage shall be paid for as fully as if the said salving ship or ships belonged to strangers. Such deposit as the carrier or his agents may deem sufficient to cover the estimated contribution of the goods and any salvage and special charges thereof shall, if required, be made by the goods, shippers, consignees or owners of the goods to the carrier before delivery.

Jerque Note. A certificate issued by the Customs Officer that he has inspected the vessel, and is assured that all cargo on board has been delivered and none remains.

Jerquer. The official of Customs who finally examines and passes the record of a ship's cargo, etc.

Jetsam. Goods which have been jettisoned, or thrown overboard, for the purpose of lightening the ship.

Jettison. To throw overboard. If the action is taken in a time of peril, and all the essentials of a general average act are present, the cargo jettisoned and any damage caused by such action is recoverable from general average.

j. & w. o. Jettison and washing overboard.

K

Kilderkin. A small barrel containing liquid measure of 18 gallons (2 firkins).

Knot. Measure of speed, being one nautical mile of 6,080 feet traversed in one hour.

L

Laden in Bulk. A shipping term used when a ship receives her cargo loose or in bulk. Cereals are often shipped in this way.

Lagen. Goods jettisoned, but a floating object is attached by which their position is marked for their subsequent recovery.

Lamcon. Iron ore charter party for ore from Liberia to all destinations.

Land Waiter. A Customs officer who tastes, weighs, measures and examines goods liable to duty, and takes an account of them, for the purpose of taxation, on their being landed from a ship; or, in the case of exported goods, who watches over and certifies that the goods are shipped in accordance with the prescribed form.

Landing Book is a book kept by dock companies and warehouse keepers in which are recorded the net and gross weights, the description and exact condition of goods as they are landed and received on their wharves.

Landing Order. Authority to the dock company or wharfinger, to receive goods from the ship.

Landing Weight. The actual weight of goods on their being landed from a ship.

L.A.S.H. Lighter-aboard-ship.

Latent Defect. Some hidden defect in machinery or equipment which is not discernible by exterior or ordinary examination.

Lawful Merchandise. Any cargo which is not carried in contravention of the laws of the country. The expression frequently occurs in time charter parties when limits of type of cargo to be carried during the contract are to be set out.

Lay Days. Days allowed for the loading or discharge of a vessel, as stipulated in the charter party. Certain days may be apportioned for the separate actions of loading and discharge. If a total number of days is stated for both operations, such days then are known as reversible lay days.

Lazaretto. The part of the ship in which persons under quarantine regulations are quartered, or the place where goods are fumigated.

L.C. London clause, which reads as follows:—" The shipowner shall be entitled to land these goods on the quays or the dock when steamer discharges immediately on arrival, and upon the goods being so landed the shipowner's responsibility ceases. This clause is to form part of the bill of lading and any words at variance with it are hereby cancelled."

L.C.L. Less than Container Load. A small consignment insufficient to utilize a container. This may use the groupage system.

Leadage. The cost of transporting minerals to the port of loading.

L.E.F.O. Lands End for Orders.

Letter of Credit. See Credit.

Letter of Hypothecation. The letter of authority given to a bank under a documentary credit whereby the bank is authorized to dispose of the goods if the consignee fails to meet his commitments. Unless the bank receives a letter of hypothecation, it has no rights in the goods as holder of a bill of exchange.

Letter of Indemnity. A letter which holds the recipient absolved from responsibility for certain eventualities. Such a letter may be given against lost documents, etc., and acted upon with confidence. It is made doubly reliable if countersigned by the bank. Letters of indemnity for clean bills of lading (q.v.) should be dealt with only as a matter of "good faith."

Letter of Marque (or Mart). A Government licence given to the owners of private ships during the time of war, commissioning them to attack and seize the ships or property of the enemy. This licence becomes redundant under modern conditions where the Government requisitions all tonnage into its own control.

Levant. Eastern end of the Mediterranean, including the islands.

Lien. The right acquired by Common Law, and backed by possession, of holding goods until a debt due in respect of such goods is satisfied. A general lien occurs when the carrier extends, by the terms of his contract, his right to hold any of the cargo owner's goods against the settlement of any outstanding charges. A maritime lien works in reverse to a normal lien. See also **Maritime Lien, General Lien, Possessory Lien,** and **Compulsory Sale.**

Light Dues. Tolls levied on vessels for the purpose of maintaining lighthouses and lightships and buoys around the coast. Dues are calculated upon the ship's registered tonnage, plus deck cargo tonnage if any is being carried. See also **Trinity House.**

Lighterage. The charge made for the use of a barge or lighter.

Limitation of Shipowner's Liability. The limitation which may be granted by the Courts to a shipowner, whereby, in certain circumstances, his limit of liability is set at 3,100 gold francs per ton. Of this figure 1,000 gold francs is set aside for cargo claims. These limitations are covered by Sects. 502–509 of the Merchant Shipping Act, 1894, as amended by subsequent statutes. The provisions are unaffected by the terms of the Carriage of Goods by the Sea Act, 1924. For calculation into sterling equivalents, the following values are laid down by Statute.

$$3,100 \text{ gold francs} = £73.4416$$
$$1,000 \text{ gold francs} = £23.6941$$

Liner. Any vessel which operates as a unit in a regular service between ports.

Linertime. Baltic and International Maritime Conference Deep Sea Time Charter Party 1968.

Litre. A metric liquid measure equalling 1.75980 pints.

Lloyd's. The premier marine insurance market of the world controlled by the Corporation of Lloyd's. Strict financial regulations govern the Underwriters who comprise the membership of the Corporation. All transactions at Lloyd's must be conducted through a recognized broker. Insurances other than marine risks are also dealt with at Lloyd's.

Lloyd's Agent. Agent of the Corporation of Lloyd's.

Lloyd's Average Bond. See **Average Bond.**

Lloyd's Register of Shipping. British ship classification society. This society is a distinct organization, and is not part of the Corporation of Lloyd's.

Lloyd's Surveyor. The surveyor employed by *Lloyd's Register of Shipping.*

L.L.T. London landed terms. See **L.C.**

L.M.C. Lloyd's Machinery Certificate. Certificate issued by *Lloyd's Register* when the ship's machinery conforms to the requirements of the Society.

L.M.C. CS (date). The Lloyd's machinery certificate notation in *Lloyd's Register* issued to ships with oil engines which are under continuous survey arrangements.

Load. Load of round timber is 40 cu. ft. Load of square timber is 50 cu. ft. Load of bricks is 500 bricks.

Loading Brokers. Brokers or agents engaged by the shipowner to attend to the loading and documentary work connected with the despatch of a vessel.

Loading turn. Rotation in order for ships to berth and load cargo.

Loadline. The mark on the ship's side showing the maximum permitted loaded draught of the vessel. The position of the mark is established by a loadline committee, and is variable according to zones of trading and season of the year by the grid marking at side.

Loco. Cost of the goods at place of purchase, *i.e.* " ex warehouse."

Log-Book. A book kept by the captain on board ship in which he records the vessel's daily progress, the winds, weather, and anything of interest which occurs to her, or on board, during the voyage. Separate log-books are kept by " deck " and " engine " departments of the ship. See also **Official Log.**

London Clause. See **L.C.**

Long Room. Upper Hall in Custom House where Customs papers relative to the clearance of goods and ships are lodged.

Long Ton. 2,240 lb.

Lord Campbell's Act. Popular name for the Fatal Accidents Act of 1846, by which dependants of a deceased person have the right to maintain an action for the loss suffered by them.

LT. LF. LS. LW. and LWNR. Timber marking on the loadline grid applicable to ships with wood cargoes. See **Loadline.**

L.W.O.S.T. Low water, ordinary spring tide.

M

Managing Owner. Person appointed by the owners to arrange all matters concerning the ship. Generally he is one of the part owners of the vessel. As the part owners are tenants in common and not partners, it is easier for a managing owner to deal with the business instead of having to obtain majority decisions from the part owners. Where a person other then a part owner is appointed, he is known as the " Ship's Husband."

Manifest. A specification of all cargo on board the ship. This document contains details of marks, numbers, contents, shipper, consignee, and such other details as may be required by Customs or consular authorities. Copies of manifests are provided for the country of export and country of import Customs authorities. The manifest of cargo on board a ship outwards from the United Kingdom must be lodged with the Statistics Dept. of the Customs within six days of vessel's departure.

Marine Insurance. A contract by which a collective number of individuals, called underwriters, or certain public companies, engage to indemnify the owner of a ship, cargo or freight against losses incident to marine adventure.

Maritime Lien. A lien upon the ship's tackle, ship, or cargo for outstanding charges. Such a lien attaches to the object upon which the charge is raised, and possession is therefore not necessary. The holder of a maritime lien has the right of instituting an enforced sale to recover his charges. Maritime liens attach in the reverse order to normal liens, *e.g.* a later lien takes precedence over earlier liens for repayment.

Markings of a British Ship. Every ship must be marked with its name on each side of the bows and on stern, port of Registry on stern, scale of feet on stem and either side of sternpost, official number on main beam, and loadline marking, the position of which is allotted individually to each ship. See also **Plimsoll Mark.**

Master (or Shipmaster). Correct term applied to the officer in charge of a merchant ship, (M.S. Act, Sect. 742). The term " captain " is purely a courtesy title. The master has (M.S. Act, Sect. 167) the same rights and remedies as a seaman, except where a pledge of the ship under bottomry has taken place.

Master Porter. A person licensed by the various dock companies and harbour boards to attend to the receiving, weighing, and sorting of goods, or the proper discharge of vessels upon their arrival in port.

Master's Declaration Outwards. Declaration by the master that the particulars on the declaration regarding the ship are correct and in accordance with M.S. Act requirements. If the ship is in ballast a " Declaration Outwards (in ballast) " is given.

Mate. The deputy who takes the command of a ship in the absence of the master. This term is usually applied to the chief or first officer of the ship.

Mate's Receipt. See **M/R.**

Mauritanore. Baltic and International Maritime Conference Charter Party 1962 for ore from Mauritania only.

M.B.S. Machinery classification in *Lloyd's Register* indicating that machinery was classified according to British Corporation Rules.

Mean Nautical Mile. Distance of 6076.91 feet.

Measurement of cargo. Length by breadth by depth measurements give the cubic capacity of cargo. The measure is taken from extreme to extreme and includes battens, banding, etc. Goods are measured as to the space they will occupy in a ship's hold; thus barrels measure length by breadth by width at widest part. Goods which taper, as telegraph poles, are measured as stacked whereby the poles are stacked in reverse layers and one thick end of pole counters the thin end of another. Cargoes which have a tendency to vary in their cubic capacity during the voyage, such as grain which has a tendency to settle, are calculated on loaded quantities.

Medcon. Chamber of Shipping East Coast Coal Charter Party 1922, for East Coast (Humber/Berwick) to Danube and River Plate.

Meditore. Chamber of Shipping 1921 Mediterranean Ore Charter Party form.

Merseycon. Chamber of Shipping Costing Coal Charter Party 1921, for West of England Mersey district ports to United Kingdom/Continent.

Metre. 3.28084275 ft. (Cub. metre = 35.3148 cu. ft.).

Metric ton. 2204.6223 lb.

M.I. Act. Marine Insurance Act, 1906. A statute codifying and regulating the conduct of marine insurance. The Act renders void any policy of marine insurance in which the insured has not an " insurable interest " or expectation of such interest, as being in the nature of gaming or wagering.

M.I.Ex. Corporate Member of the Institute of Export.

Mille. 1,220 pieces of timber.

Misrepresentation. Certain information contained in a charter party is of such value that if it were other than absolutely correct it could affect the whole of the contract. Such information, whilst not being warranted, is held to be a representation. If the data supplied are incorrect, the charter party may be cancelled on the grounds of misrepresentation. Examples of this would be wrong details of the trading position of the vessel or of the ship's capacity.

Mole. A long pier or jetty covering the entrance to a harbour.

M/R. (Mate's Receipt). A receipt issued by the chief officer of the ship for cargo which is delivered alongside by craft. It is a temporary receipt, exchangeable in due course for the bill of lading. A mate's receipt is not negotiable but is assignable as any other chose in action. Notice of assignment is necessary to bind the shipowner.

M.S.A. Merchant Shipping Act. This term includes not only the main Act of 1894 but the many supplementary or amending acts which have since been passed.

Muster Roll. See **Crew List.**

N

n.a.a. Not always afloat. The use of the abbreviation indicates that the obligation of being " always afloat " (see **a.a.**) does not apply.

n.a.a.b.s.a. Not always afloat but safe aground.

Named Policy. A marine insurance policy in which the name of the vessel carrying the goods insured is inserted.

Name of Ship. No change of name may be made without permission of the Board of Trade. Nor may a name be changed for the purpose of deceit. Where a change has occurred *Lloyd's Register* and other Registers give all names previously held by the vessel.

Nautical Mile. Distance varying from 6045.93 ft. on equator to 6107.98 ft. in lat. 90°. A mean nautical mile is 6076.91 ft.

N.B. New boiler, notation with date of fitting, shown in *Lloyd's Register*.

n.d. Non-delivery.

n.d.b. Notation in *Lloyd's Register* of new donkey boiler, and date of fitting.

N.E. Note in *Lloyd's Register*, with date, of fitting of new engine.

Necessaries. Those things which an owner of a ship, being a prudent man, would have purchased had he been present at the time. The shipmaster has the right to pledge his owner's credit for the purchase of " necessaries." If the purchase does not come within this term the master of the ship may be liable for these on his own account.

Necore. Chamber of Shipping 1922 Mediterranean Ore Charter Party.

Negligence. Neglect to do certain things or to carry out certain precautions. Broadly speaking the loss arising through negligence is borne by the person who is neglectful, and the negligence of an agent becomes the negligence of the principal, with powers of recompense from the agent. The difficulty of setting down any certain rules on this question arises through the many degrees of negligence, *e.g.* negligence, wilful negligence, and criminal negligence. Whether an act of wilful negligence might be considered an act of barratry would depend upon circumstances.

Net or Nett weight. The weight of goods excluding exterior packing (case, etc.).

Nett nett weight. A weight which gives the actual weight of goods exclusive of exterior packing (case, etc.) and also exclusive of individual container (*e.g.* bottle, tin, carton, etc.).

Net tonnage. See **n.r.t.**

n/n. Not north of. A term used sometimes when the trading limits of a vessel (under time charter party) are defined. Also used when cases are not given individual numbers, and means, in this instance, no numbers.

n.o.p. Not otherwise provided.

Northern Range. The ports of Norfolk, Newport News, Baltimore, Philadelphia, New York, Boston, and Portland (Maine).

Notice of Abandonment. The certain and unconditional notice given by an assured to an underwriter within a reasonable time of receiving information that a loss has taken place, when he intends to abandon his interest and claim for a constructive total loss.

Notice of Readiness. The formal intimation by the shipowner to the charterer that the ship is ready to load. The tender of notice of readiness is one of the obligations necessary to make the ship an "arrived ship" (q.v.).

65

Not negotiable. When a document is "not negotiable" it means "that the receiver shall not have, and shall not be capable of giving, a better title to the document than the person from whom he received it had."

n.r.a.d. No risk after discharge. The carrier is freed of responsibility once goods are discharged from the ship.

n.r.a.l. No risk after landing. As **n.r.a.d.** with the proviso that discharge (overside) may occur some time before landing actually takes place.

n.r.a.s. No risk after shipment. The seller of goods is free of risk once the goods have been shipped.

n.r.t. Net register tonnage. This is calculated on the basis of 100 cu. ft. per ton of ship's enclosed space, after deduction from gross tonnage figures of engine and navigation spaces.

n.t. Net terms. Rates are free of charterer's commission.

Nubaltwood. Baltic Wood Charter, 1964. Baltic and Norway to U.K. and Republic of Ireland.

Nuvoy. Charter Party 1964 for trade with "Eastern Countries" where no other charter party has been issued.

O

o.a. Over all. Term used in measuring, meaning that measurement is calculated from extreme to extreme.

O/B/O. Ore/Bulk/Oil ship.

Official Log. Is the record book of ship which contains all entries of prime importance relative to the voyage.

Official Register. Ship's document of identity giving name and number of ship, rig size, registered tonnage, owners, master and port of registry. See **Certificate of Registry.**

O.G. Indication in *Lloyd's Register* that propeller shaft is sectional and junctions are fitted with oil glands.

On Passage. Grain and other produce is said to be " on passage " when the vessel carrying it is on the voyage but has not yet reached her destination.

On the Berth. A vessel loading, or ready to receive her cargo, is said to be " on the berth."

Onus of Proof. The responsibility of proof. In most circumstances the person who alleges the fault must prove the failure of the other party to take the necessary steps to prevent loss or damage. But in certain Acts, as the Carriage of Goods by Sea Act, 1924, the Act specifically provides that the onus of proof shall be on the person claiming the benefit of the Act.

Open Charter. Charter party whereby vessel may fix any cargo and for any ports.

Open Indent. An order to a supplier for goods of unspecified manufacture which enables the supplier to purchase the most suitable goods at the best obtainable price. Specified goods of a named brand would be ordered by a " closed indent."

Open Policy, a marine insurance term, means that the value is not definitely fixed but that a certain amount has been *provisionally* insured, leaving the declaration of the goods and their value to be subsequently named.

Orecon. Baltic and International Maritime Conference Charter Party 1950 for ore from Scandinavia to Poland.

Origin. See **Certificate of Origin.**

O/S/O. Ore/Slurry/Oil ship.

Outturn. The amount of cargo discharged from a ship. A daily figure, or a total figure.

Over all (or Overall). See **o.a.**

Owner's Declaration. The declaration of an owner of his right to own a share in the ship, and that no unqualified person owns a share in the ship. This is a necessary document for registration of ownership of a vessel.

P

P. Poop. Notation of a deck erection on a vessel, as shown by *Lloyd's Register*. The poop is situated at the stern.

Packing. Dependent on the nature of the cargo, goods will be deemed "insufficiently packed" if the shipowner deems the containers not suitable for the hazards anticipated. An insufficiency of packing clause renders the bill a "dirty" bill.

P.A. Particular average. A partial loss of the subject matter insured caused by a peril insured against, and which is not a general average loss.

Panamax. Maximum size permitted Panama Canal.

Panstone. Chamber of Shipping 1920 Stone Charter Party form.

Particular Average. See **P.A.**

Passenger List. The document which contains names and details of passengers on board the vessel. This list is required both by emigration authorities at port of embarkation, and immigration authorities at port of destination.

Passport. See **Ship's Passport.**

Payload. The carrying capacity of a container.

Penalty (for non-fulfilment). The penalty stipulated in a charter party is limited to an amount not exceeding gross estimated amount of freight. Such a provision should be read as " proved damages," for there can arise only an action for damages and never one for enforcement of a penalty.

Perfecting the sight. Completion of the details unknown at the time of lodging a bill of sight (q.v.).

Perils of the Sea (and navigable waters). Perils which are to be encountered on the voyage, which are peculiar to the sea. Such an expression does not include the normal action of the wind and waves.

per mille. Per thousand. Is often written $^\circ/_{\circ\circ}$.

P. & I. Protection and indemnity.

Pilot. The authorized person employed in navigating a vessel safely into or out of a port. Trinity House is the pilotage authority for the United Kingdom. Pilots will operate as river pilots or deep sea pilots. Dock pilots operating inside the dock are usually part of the dock organization, and do not come within the Trinity House authority. The M.S. Act, Sect. 742, defines a pilot as any person not belonging to a ship who has the conduct thereof. All pilots must hold certificates of authority, which are renewable annually, and are governed by the terms of the Pilotage Act, 1913.

Pilotage. Payment made for the services of a pilot, or the actual service itself.

Piracy. Acts of robbery and violence committed on the high seas by one vessel against another.

Pitwoodcon. Chamber of Shipping Pitwood Charter Party 1924 France to Bristol Channel.

Pix-Pinus. Chamber of Shipping Pitch Pine Charter Party 1906 from Gulf of Mexico and Central America for United Kingdom/Continent and Mediterranean trade.

Plimsoll Mark. Popular name for the loadline markings (q.v.) of a ship, perpetuating the memory of Samual Plimsoll who, in 1868, commenced agitation in Parliament for safety provisions for men at sea.

p.o.c. Port of call. A port at which a vessel is entitled to enter during the course of the given voyage.

Polcon. Baltic and International Maritime Conference Charter Party 1950 for coal and coke from Poland.

Policy Proof of Interest. See **P.P.I.**

Poop. Raised deck at stern of vessel.

p.o.r. Port of refuge. A port into which a vessel may enter when necessity arises, *e.g.* to shelter from a storm, to carry out essential repairs, etc.

Port. The left-hand side of a ship when looking towards the bow.

Portage Bill. The account of members of the crew of a vessel giving particulars of wages, allowances, etc.

Port Charges. The charge made by a port upon ship or cargo for use of the port.

Port of Entry. Port at which vessel or goods are entered (*i.e.* cleared through Customs) into or out of the country.

Port of Registry. The place where ship is registered. This must be shown on stern of vessel. The owner of the ship has free election of the port of registry, and most owners register all their fleet at the same port. All port registers are governed by the Registrar General of Shipping, and the local Registrar is the chief officer of Customs or such other person as may be appointed by Orders in Council.

Possessory Lien. A common law lien where possession of goods is necessary in order to retain the right of lien. If possession of the goods upon which the lien is enforced is lost the creditor must seek other ways of recovering his outstanding charges. A lien holder may transfer the goods to another (*e.g.* warehousekeeper) who will exercise possession on his behalf. In such cases it is necessary for the owner of the goods to pay his outstanding account plus the warehouse-keepers' charges before the goods are released. (See M.S. Act, Sect. 494.)

Post Entry. When an importer after having passed a Customs entry for goods, finds that his entry is too small, he must make a post or additional entry for the overplus.

p.p. Picked ports. Selected ports.

P.P.I. Policy proof of interest. Insurer will not dispute the assured's right of insurable interest in the event of a loss arising.

Pratique. The permit for a vessel to communicate with land after a clean bill of health has been produced, or quarantine restrictions have been observed. This is completed by the Medical Officer and states the name of the ship, name of master and port from which vessel has arrived.

Prima facie. On the face of it; at the first glance.

Primage. Percentage added to freight, and retained by the shipowner until such time as it is recovered in part, or as a whole as a rebate according to the regulations of the conference under which the vessel is operating. Originally primage was a payment made by shippers to provide funds to assist the shipowner in meeting disbursement before freight was earned. Subsequently it became a payment to the master for his personal care of the cargo, and later it became the means of ensuring the regular patronage of shippers to the regular lines even if opposition ships were available at lower rates of freight. In later years the primage charge and the rebate have been abandoned by many companies, and superseded by a 'contract' which the shipper signs to send all his cargoes by conference vessels.

Proceed with all despatch. Obligation upon a vessel to go on her journey by the quickest possible recognized route at her best speed.

Pro forma. As a matter of form.

Pro rata. Proportionately. The expression " pro rata freight " can apply only when the shipper agrees to take delivery of his cargo at an intermediate port. Freight, unless otherwise specified, is payable in full for the whole voyage and is either earned or not earned. Freight contracts are not made on a " quantum meruit " basis.

Propcon. Baltic and International Maritime Conference Charter Party 1937 for props and pulpwood from Baltic and Norway to Continent.

Protest. Declaration, on oath, by the master of a ship giving particulars of bad weather encountered on the voyage, date of leaving port, and date of arrival. Protest may be made by master if charterer contravenes charter party terms, or for charges which have been levied at an excess price.

Provisional Certificate. The provisional certificate of registry granted by the British Consular Office following the purchase of a ship abroad, for use until ship is registered with the Registrar General of Shipping.

p.r.p. Proper return port. The port to which the seaman must be returned at the expense of the owners, when his engagement is terminated.

Public Enemies. Persons who operate against the written or unwritten laws of the people, *e.g.* pirates, outlaws, etc.

Public Policy. The conditions operating by the will of rulers or peoples which are introduced for benefit of all sections of the community.

Puncheon. A liquid measure which contains 72 gallons, or it may vary in quantity up to 120 gallons.

Q

Q. Note in *Lloyd's Register* that ship's engines are quadruple engines.

Quantum Meruit. " As much as he deserves " the principle of payment for work done as opposed to payment for a completed task.

Quarantine Restrictions. The restrictions imposed by health authorities for the isolation of infectious and contagious diseases. A ship is placed in quarantine by segregation from other ships, and is allowed no communication with the shore, or entry into the port until the Medical Officer is satisfied that the danger is past.

Quebec Standard. 229¼ cu. ft. of timber.

Queen's Enemies. Declared enemies of the State.

R

Ratification. The act of authorizing an agent's actions some time after he has carried out his tasks without authority.

r.d. Running days. Consecutive days calculated without reference to Sundays, holidays, etc.

r.d.c. Running down clause. A clause which may be incorporated into a policy insuring the hull of the ship. Briefly it is part provision against the liability for which the insured ship may be held responsible as the result of a collision.

Rebate. Rebate of freight is given to a regular shipper on Conference Line vessels who does not patronize non-conference vessels during a given period of time. (See **Primage.**) This has in many cases been superseded by a contract system.

Received Bill of Lading. A Bill of Lading which only acknowledges that goods have been received for shipment, and does not state that goods are shipped. There is no difference in value at law, although some banks will not accept received bills in support of documentary bills. The matter is fully covered in the Carriage of Goods by Sea Act, 1924, Art. 3. (7) wherein the shipper is entitled to demand a shipped bill when the goods are loaded on board.

Receiving Note. In the shipment of goods, a note, forming part of the shipping notes addressed by the shipper to the chief officer of a ship, asking him to receive on board the goods therein specified.

Recta. Bill of Lading. A bill of lading where delivery is restricted to the named consignee. The clause " o/order or their assigns " is deleted from the bill.

Reefer Space. An expression sometimes used to indicate the refrigerated cargo space of a vessel.

Ref. Notation in *Lloyd's Register* that ship is fitted with refrigeration machinery.

Registered Ship. In compliance with the Merchant Shipping Act, all ships over 15 tons, except river and coastal craft and excluding ships up to 30 tons fishing or trading in Newfoundland, must be registered with the Registrar General of Shipping.

Registered tonnage. See **Gross Tonnage** and **n.r.t.**

Regular turn. When vessels take precedence for loading or discharge in proper rotation. Time commences to count only when vessel has arrived at the berth.

Report. The report of the ship to Customs giving details of ship, tonnage, crew, port from which vessel has arrived, particulars of cargo and consignees. Where a ship is reporting in ballast, the word " Ballast " should be entered in space for cargo details.

Representation. See under **Misrepresentation.**

Request Note is a special permit from the Customs to land perishable or other goods before the ship has reported and cleared at the Custom House.

Re-rummaged. A ship is rummaged while discharging her cargo, and re-rummaged when taking in her export cargo. See **Rummaged, Rummaging.**

Respondentia. The pledging of a cargo in order to raise funds to enable the ship to reach her destination. The holder of the respondentia bond has a lien on the cargo which becomes void should the vessel be lost. The bondholder, therefore, has an insurable interest in his loan.

Restraint of Princes, Rulers and Peoples. Embargos upon the movements of ships or cargoes instigated by the country concerned. The wording of the phrase includes Monarchies, Parliaments, Senates, dictatorships, and *de facto* governments.

Return. Alternative term for "Tally" (q.v.).

Return Premium. A return of premium payable by an insurer to an insured.

Reversible Lay Days. See **Lay Days.**

Riggers. Men engaged to rig ships with working gear for stevedores to load or discharge cargoes.

River Dues. The charges imposed by a river authority for the use, by the ship, of the river.

Road or Roadstead. A place where ships can ride at anchor at some distance from the shore.

Ro Ro. Roll on, Roll off ship.

Rules of Practice. Rules of practice of the Association of Average Adjusters for the adjustment of particular and general average.

Rummaged. A ship is said to be " rummaged " after she has been properly searched by the Custom House officials.

Rummaging. The searching of a ship by the Custom House officers to see that neither dutiable nor prohibited goods are concealed on board.

Runners. Men engaged to shift a vessel from one port to another; for example, a vessel discharging in London and loading in Liverpool would engage runners to transfer the ship, and thus obviate the necessity of signing on a crew in London. Pay for this work is supplemented by the men's expenses for returning to their original port.

Running Days. A chartering term for consecutive days, including Sundays; the ship, therefore, not being limited to working days.

Running-down Clause. A clause inserted in a marine insurance policy by which underwriters agree to pay certain damages caused by the ship, whose insurance they have undertaken, in the event of her collision with another vessel.

Russcon. Chamber of Shipping Grain Charter Party form 1912 for Black Sea berth contracts.

Rye Terms. " R.T.F.O. Rye terms full outturn " means that Rye is purchased on the quantity delivered. " R.T.S.D. Rye terms sound delivered " means that Rye is bought on condition of sound delivery.

S

S. The Summer marking to be found on the Loadline Grid.

s.a. Subject to approval.

Sabotage. Wilful destruction, or obstruction resulting in delay sufficient to destroy contemplated objective.

Safe Port. A port in which a vessel and her cargo can lie without interference from physical or political causes.

Sailing Cards are cards issued by ship brokers to their customers, giving particulars of the ship, or ships they are about to load, the loading berth, date of departure, destination, etc.

Sailing Telegram. The advice from a shipowner to the charterer when the vessel leaves her last port of discharge. This notice is an obligation under the charter party agreement, and gives the charterer time to make arrangements for the loading of his cargo.

Sale of Goods Act. An Act of 1894 which codified the law relating to the Sale of Goods in relation to formation, effect and performance of the contract, rights of seller and breach of contract.

Saltcon. Baltic and International Maritime Conference Charter Party 1947 for salt from Mediterranean to Norway. And for other salt cargoes.

Salvage may mean:—
1. Money paid to those who assist in saving a ship or goods from the dangers of the sea;
2. The goods so saved;
3. Property saved from a fire on land.

Salvage Loss. A marine insurance term for a loss settled by underwriters after a certain sum representing the value of goods saved has been deducted from the amount for which the goods were insured.

s.a.n.r.   Subject to approval no risk.

s.b.s.   Surveyed before shipment.   Goods are examined before they are loaded on board the vessel.

Scale of feet.   Every British ship must *inter alia* be marked on the stem and sternpost with a scale of feet for clear indication of draught.   Failure to comply brings a liability of £100.

Scale of Provisions.   The scale of provisions as set out by the Board of Trade, which the shipowner is bound to supply for crews.   The Merchant Shipping Act, 1970, lays down procedure for complaints and the master's liability for non compliance.

Scancon.   Baltic and Mercantile International Conference Charter Party 1956 for Scandinavian trades where no other Charter Party is in force.

Scanorecon.   Baltic and International Maritime Conference General Ore Charter Party 1962.

Scuttle.   To let water into a ship for the purpose of sinking.

Seabee.   Similar to **L.A.S.H.**, but handling big barges twice the size of previously.

Seaman.   Every person (excluding masters, pilots, and apprentices) employed on board a ship.

Seaman's Lien.   Every seaman has the right to invoke a maritime lien upon the ship for non-payment of wages, (Sect. 167, M.S. Act).   Liens for wages take priority over other liens for payment.

Searchers.   The Customs officials whose duty it is to see that the exportation of goods takes place according to the prescribed routine; who issue the documents allowing the shipment of dutiable goods, whether as cargo or stores.

Seaworthiness. The fitness of a vessel to withstand the anticipated perils of the voyage, and to carry out safely the obligations of the contract. Such a contract must not be an impossibility (*Esposito* v. *Bowden*, 1857).

In a charter party the shipowner warrants a good ship, and in the event of a loss the onus of proving unseaworthiness is upon the claimant.

In shipments under the Carriage of Goods by Sea Act, the carrier is bound before and at the beginning of every voyage to exercise due diligence to make the ship seaworthy, to properly man, equip and supply the vessel, and to make the holds, refrigerating and cool chambers, and all other parts of the ship in which goods are carried, fit and safe for their reception, carriage, and preservation. In the event of a claim arising for unseaworthiness, the onus of proof rests upon the shipowner to show his exercise of due diligence.

Set of Bills of Lading. A set of bills of lading must contain at least one negotiable bill of lading, and one non-negotiable "master's" copy. If more than one negotiable bill is issued, then the master or person signing will affirm the number of bills stating that "the first of which being accomplished the others stand void." The number of negotiable bills and non-negotiable copies will vary according to the requirements of consular authorities, and the shippers' own needs.

S/H.E. or SHEX. Sundays and holidays excepted. An expression contained in the charter party with regard to the computation of time for loading or discharge. Where the term "Forward Sundays and holidays to count" is met with, this provides that a vessel may claim despatch money upon all the time saved. For example, a vessel may complete discharge at noon on Saturday, whereas loading time is calculated to noon on Monday. Time saved is 48 hours and not the four loading hours of Monday only.

Shelter Deck Steamer. A vessel which has a higher super-structure deck above the main deck of the vessel. Under a recent IMCO recommendation the tendency is for the tonnage opening not to be cut in the upper deck or, if fitted, to be permanently closed. A new tonnage mark indicates, when submerged, that the ship is sailing in what used to be the 'closed' or C.S.D. condition and is rated at her full tonnage. When the tonnage mark is not submerged she is rated at the lower or O.S.D. tonnages.

Shifting Boards. Wood partitions which are erected in a ship's hold for the purpose of breaking up fluid cargoes such as grain in bulk. These boards separate the hold into sections, and any change of level caused by heavy movement of the ship due to bad weather does not affect stability or cause the ship to list. By international agreement shifting boards for bulk grain shipments are compulsory unless alternative arrangements are nationally approved.

SHINC. Sundays and holidays included.

Ship. A ship is a vessel of any description used in navigation and not propelled by oars whether completed or in the course of completion. This definition (given in Sect. 742 of the M.S. Act) is not of a limiting nature but an extended description.

Ship Brokers. Agents appointed by the owners to transact the business of ships, and obtain cargo and passengers.

Shipmaster. See Master.

Shipowner. Any person who is entitled to be registered as the owner of one or more shares in a ship. A ship is divided into 64/64th shares which may be held by:—

Natural born British subjects,

Naturalized British subjects,

Citizens by letter of denizenship,

Body corporate with its principal office in some part of H.M. Dominions (Sect. 1, Merchant Shipping Act, 1894).

All part-owners of a ship are tenants in common, and not partners. A majority decision regulates the employment of the vessel unless management is given to a managing owner or ship's husband. Where an engagement is arranged against the wishes of the minority, a suitable indemnity must be given by the majority against the safe return of the vessel. If the ship is lost, the minority is recompensed, but if she returns they do not share in the profits of the voyage. (*In re Blanchard* 1923.)

Shipped Bill of Lading. A bill of Lading which contains the statement that goods have been " shipped." The shipper may demand a shipped bill under his rights as contained in the Carriage of Goods by Sea Act, 1924.

Shipping Bills are:—
1. Customs documents used in cases where drawback is claimed upon dutiable goods transhipped either for re-export or for use on board during the voyage.
2. Documents giving particulars of the goods and exporting vessel, used chiefly for statistical purposes.

Shipping Note. The advice which is sent by the shipper to the wharfinger containing details of marks, numbers, number of packages, weight measurement, and port of destination. Upon receipt of the returned note signed by the wharfinger, the shipper lodges bills of lading knowing that goods will invariably be shipped. The use of shipping notes is not operative at all ports.

Ship's Agreement. See **Crew Agreement.**

Ship's Husband. See **Managing Owner.**

Ship's Official Number. The official number allocated to a ship upon registration. This number remains unaltered throughout the life of the vessel and is her identity number. This number should be cut or punched on to the main beam of the vessel, but when this is inaccessible it is customary to have the number stamped on the after end of the forward hatch coamings.

Ship's Papers. These consist of a ship's certificate of registry, her manifest, muster roll, charter party (if any), bill of health (if required), log book, the crew agreement, and bills of lading.

Ship's Passport. A document given to the captain of a neutral ship in times of war, as his authority to proceed on a voyage, and also to prove the vessel's nationality.

Ship's Rail. Expression sometimes found in documents meaning that ship's liability shall cease when goods pass " over the ship's rail." The literal interpretation of this is incorrect. Once the shipowner commences to load the cargo he is responsible for its care, and in the same way his liability is continued in discharge until the goods have been safely landed. Landing, according to custom, may be into barge, on to quay, or in some other specified manner.

Short Delivery. Cargo delivered short of the quantity stated in the bill of lading.

Short Shipment. Goods are said to be a short shipment, or short shipped, when part is not loaded.

Short Ton. A ton of 2,000 lb.

Shut out. When a consigment or part consignment is awaiting shipment but not loaded on board owing to the ship being full, or vessel having to sail before all cargo is put on board.

Signal Letters. The signal letters allocated to a ship by international agreement and used where necessary for signalling between ship and ship, or ship and shore.

Signature of Charter Parties. When a charter party is signed by a broker on behalf of the principal, it is essential that such a signature should be clearly qualified. The words "agent" or "as agent," are insufficient to secure freedom from liability by the broker of his principal's obligations. Should the principal withdraw, the broker may be held to be principal to the contract and therefore obliged to complete the agreement. The broker should, therefore, qualify his signature "as agent for charterer." Where a charter is fixed subject to certain provisions, the use of a further qualification, *e.g.* "By Telegraphic Authority" or "Subject to Owner's Approval" should be added if permissible.

Signing on or off of crews. The action of the shipmaster in opening or closing the ship's agreement with the crew.

Single Deck Ship. A ship fitted with one deck only.

Skids. Beams on which containers are mounted to facilitate loading and discharge.

Slatings. Wood measuring from ¾ in. to 1 in. thick, from 1 in. to 2 in. wide, and more than 5 ft. long.

Slinging. A shipping term used in some ports in the kingdom; it means a charge for putting the chains round the goods as they lie in craft alongside a ship, so that the vessel may hoist them on board. It is usually borne by the shipper.

Sovcoal. Coal and Coke and Coal Tar Pitch Charter Party 1962 from Russia.

Sovietwood. Chamber of Shipping charter party 1961 for Sovietwood to the United Kingdom, Ireland and other countries.

Spanfrucon. Baltic and International Maritime Conference Charter Party 1926 for fruit from Spain to European ports.

Special Stowage. Goods which are of a hazardous nature may be required to have special attention and placed in a part of the ship where they will not affect the other cargo. The hazard may arise through the cargo having a flash point, or where the nature of the cargo may be ranked as "dirty," i.e. having an odour which may cause contamination of other cargo. Under the Merchant Shipping (Dangerous Goods) Rules, 1952, declaration has to be made classifying the cargo into one of ten categories ranging from explosives to medicinal preparations.

Special Survey. A special survey prescribed by the classification society, according to their rules. May be held at four, eight, and twelve year intervals after building date.

Spot. Ready to load.

Spt. When appearing in *Lloyd's Register* after the description of main boilers, this indicates that a superheater is fitted.

Standard. A timber measure of 165 cu. ft. is known as the St. Petersburg standard. Weight varies between 2¾ and 4 tons, according to timber and seasoning. A standard should

stow between 220 and 270 cu. ft. A steamer's bale capacity
divided by 220 gives the approximate standard capacity of
the ship.

Standard Charter Party forms. The recommended forms
drawn up by the documentary committees of such organ-
izations as the Chamber of Shipping, Baltic and White Sea
Conference, etc. These forms contain suggested terms which
may be altered according to the wishes of the contracting
parties.

Starboard. The right-hand side of a ship when looking
towards the bow.

Statute Adult. The term used in calculating the number of
passengers carried on board a ship, and means any person
over twelve years of age. Two persons between the age of
one year and twelve years count as one statute adult. Children
under one year are not counted in the calculation.

Steamer's Bag. The ship's private mail bag into which is
accepted any letter from a shipper to his consignee enclosing
documents which are required on arrival of the ship. All
such letters must conform to current postal regulations. Use
of the steamer's bag has been largely superseded where air
mails operate on the same route.

Stemming. The act of booking a ship for bunkers. When
arrangements are complete, vessel is said to be " Stemmed."

Stevedore. Person who acts as a contractor for labour in
loading or discharging vessels in port.

Stiffening Order. A permission granted by the Customs for
a vessel to take in heavy goods by way of ballast to steady her
in the water, in cases where the safety of the ship requires it,
previous to authority being given for her general loading.

Stoppage in Transitu. The right of an unpaid seller or shipper to stop goods in transit from reaching the buyer or consignee who is insolvent. The rights of the seller cease on termination of the voyage, or if the buyer has sold to a bona fide purchaser and bill of lading has been assigned absolutely.

Stores List. List of stores and equipment on board ship which is prepared and handed to Customs officials at port on arrival.

Stowage Order. Instructions to the shipper of goods of an obnoxious or harmful nature which authorize him to send such cargo to the vessel for shipment. Date of shipment is stated so that special arrangements can be made to handle and stow without interference with ordinary goods. The ship's officer receives a duplicate which often includes stowage instructions. There are now specified classes of Hazardous cargo which the shipper must declare in his application for a stowage order.

Stowage Plan. Outline plan of ship on which details of cargo loaded are entered. This enables the stevedore discharging the cargo to make his arrangements for labour, etc., according to the disposition of the stowage.

Stranded. A marine insurance term for the running of a ship on a rock, a sandbank, or on shore, and remaining stationary there for any length of time, the length of time is not specific. See **Aground.**

Strike. A concerted refusal and abstention from work. Not confined to wage disputes.

Stripping. Devanning or emptying containers.

Stuffing. Loading containers.

87

Sufferance Wharf. A wharf licensed by the Customs (and at which a Custom House officer attends) where certain goods may be landed and cleared.

Supercargo. Person engaged on a vessel for the purpose of superintending the cargo, its stowage and care, to the best advantage.

T

T. Indication in *Lloyd's Register* that ship's engines are triple-expansion. Also the tropical mark of the loadline grid.

Tally. The record taken by a tally clerk of details of cargo loaded or discharged. Marks, numbers, weight, measurement and condition of the packages are included.

Tallying. The act of checking goods loaded on, or discharged from, a ship.

t. and p. Theft and pilferage.

t. and s. Touch and stay. Expression in a marine insurance policy which gives permission for the ship to call at her normal ports of call on the voyage even though the ports are unspecified.

Tanker. A vessel specially constructed and fitted for the carriage of bulk cargoes of a liquid nature, *e.g.* petroleum and molasses.

Tariff. List of duties chargeable on goods. List of freight rates issued by a shipping conference.

Telegraphic Authority. Authority granted to an agent by telegraphic means. It is essential in all cases for the agent to secure written confirmation, and to qualify his signature on any document as " by telegraphic authority." If he fails to do this, a mutilation of the message may result in the authority of his principal being exceeded and his right of passing responsibility back made void.

Telegraphic Transfer. The method by which sums of money can be transmitted to places abroad, subject to financial arrangements in force at the time. The facilities provided enable a shipmaster or agent to be placed in funds without having to pledge the ship under bottomry or respondentia.

T.F. Tropical Fresh marking of the loadline grid.

Through Bill of Lading. A bill of lading which covers not only the sea voyage but also a period of transit before the goods are loaded, or subsequent to their discharge. The shipowner will charge an inclusive rate of freight for the whole transit but states that the transit period other than the actual sea voyage is " at ship's expense but at shipper's risk."

" Ticket." The popular title for the certificate of a ship's master or officer. It is an obligation for every officer except the master to hold a certificate from the Board of Trade for one rank higher than his serving rank, *e.g.* second officer must hold a first officer's certificate. The master often holds an extra-master's certificate.

Tierce. A barrel containing 42 gallons.

" Tight Staunch and fit." Condition in the contract of affreightment that vessel is in every way fitted and seaworthy for the voyage in prospect.

Time Charter Party. Agreement for the hire of a ship for a stated period of time. The contract usually allows for the conveyance of any lawful merchandise, and limits of trading areas are broadly specified as " worldwide radius, icebound ports excepted." For the purpose of preservation of rights, the shipowner will, by the terms of the contract, provide master and chief engineer during the tenure of the contract.

T.L. Total loss. There is total loss when the subject matter is destroyed, or so damaged that it loses its original nature; where the owner is irretrieveably deprived of the subject matter.

T.L.O. Total loss only. Indicates that the underwriter pays for only a total loss, and not for a partial loss.

Ton by ton delivered. Expression used in the stipulation of freight payments for some cargoes. It has the same value as "freight paid concurrent with discharge," when freight is paid daily according to outturn figures. At all times outstanding freight figures should be compared with cargo on board in order to ensure that at no time is the lien for freight impaired.

Tonnage. A ship's carrying capacity; the number of tons she can carry. Measured in 40 cu. ft. or 20 cwts. Or, the measurement of the ship itself in units of 100 cu. ft. (See also **Gross Tonnage** and **n.r.t.**)

Tonnage dues. Dues charged on the registered tonnage of a ship and used for the maintenance of buoys, etc.

Tonnage Slip. Details of the amount of tonnage dues payable are entered on a tonnage slip and lodged with Customs at time of a clearance inwards.

Tons Burden. A ship's carrying capacity measured in tons of 40 cu. ft.

Tramp. A vessel engaged in casual trade, or upon charter party fixtures, each of which operates as a separate voyage and does not constitute part of a regular service.

Transhipment. The removal of goods from one vessel to another, or carriage from port of discharge to a final destination.

Transhipment Bond Note. This forms an entry for the goods when dutiable goods are transhipped, and states that the party named has given security for the due transhipment and exportation of the goods named therein.

Transhipment Delivery Order. A note used when dutiable goods are to be transhipped. It is addressed by the Customs to their officer on board the incoming vessel instructing him to send up in charge of an officer of Customs, to be delivered into the custody of the proper officer at the docks where the export steamer is lying, the goods specified therein.

Transhipment Entry. The Customs entry necessary for goods which are to be transhipped to another country.

Transhipment Shipping Bill forms the export entry for goods transhipped under bond. It is passed in the Long Room, and then goes to the officer in charge of the export ship, who certifies to the shipment, and takes a mate's receipt for the goods on board.

Transire. These are duplicate accounts used in the coasting trade upon the prescribed form, signed by the master of a coaster before leaving the place of loading, describing the quantities of the various goods he has taken on board.

Transitime. Chamber of Shipping Charter Party for Time Charter Fixtures.

Tret. Allowance for ordinary wear and tear or depreciation during transportation.

Trinity House. This establishment superintends the interests of British navigation and shipping by erecting beacons or lighthouses, appointing pilots, conducting the examination of mariners, and regulating to a great extent the marine interests of the country.

Truss. A bundle of straw (36 lb.) or of hay (56 lb.).

Tween Decker Ship. A ship which has an additional deck below the main deck of the vessel.

T.W.H.D. Tons per workable hatch per day.

Tr. Notation in *Lloyd's Register* that vessel is a triple-screw ship. T. indicates Twin Screw vessels.

U

U.K.F.O. United Kingdom for Orders. Vessel is to proceed to the United Kingdom, where orders for ports of discharge will be given.

Ullage. Quantity which a cask lacks of being full. This may arise because of natural evaporation, seepage, or through abstraction.

Unclean Bill of Lading. A bill of lading which has some qualifying clause to the " apparent good order and condition " of the consignment. This may be of the nature of *e.g.* "Old case renailed," " Case stained," " Unprotected," etc. Letters of indemnity given for a clean bill are of no legal value, *e.g.* conniving the issue of a document of title misrepresenting goods as stated, but such letters are used and their value is dependent upon the good faith of the person giving indemnity. These are also known as " back-letters."

Under Deck Tonnage. The measurement of space enclosed in the ship, below the main deck, calculated in tons of 100 cu. ft.

Underwriter. An insurer of ships, so called because he underwrites or subscribes his name to each policy he is concerned in.

Unseaworthy. See **Seaworthiness.**

V

Valued Policy. A marine insurance policy wherein the amount insured is valued or fixed. See **Open Policy.**

Vanning. Loading or stuffing containers.

Vessel. See **Ship.**

Vice propre. Inherent vice (q.v.).

Victualling Bill. This contains details of bonded stores taken on board the ship, but does not include the surplus stores which were on board on arrival.

Voyage Charter Party. Agreement for the hire of a vessel for the carriage of specific goods, between certain ports.

W.   Winter marking of loadline grid.

W.A.   With average.   The insurer pays claims for partial losses.

Warehousing Entry.   Document necessary before goods can be placed in a bonded warehouse.

Warranty of Seaworthiness.   The warranty or guarantee given by the shipowner that his vessel is seaworthy, *i.e.* in every way fitted for the voyage.   Such a warranty is contained in the bill of lading or charter party, in the expression " Good Ship."   The Carriage of Goods by Sea Act, 1924, provides that there shall be no warranty of seaworthiness for shipments within the scope of the Act, but the shipowner shall, before and at the beginning of the voyage, exercise due diligence to provide a seaworthy ship.   This change in the law made it no longer necessary for the shipper to disprove the shipowner's warranty (as he still is obliged to do in respect of shipments under charter parties and shipments outside the Act), but the shipowner himself is bound to prove exercise of due diligence to provide such a ship.

w.b.   Water ballast.

W.C.E.   West Coast of England.

W.C.S.A.   West Coast South America.

Weather Working Days.   Days on which work may be carried out without interference from the weather.   When work is held up by bad weather it is essential that the charterer is ready and prepared to load (or discharge) if he is to claim for time lost due to bad weather.

Weight Note. A document issued by the dock authorities giving the gross weight, tare, and net weight, the marks, numbers, and dates of entry of imported goods.

Welcon. Chamber of Shipping Coal Charter Party Form 1913 for Coasting Bristol Channel—Elbe/Brest and United Kingdom.

Welsh Coal 1896 Charter. Chamber of Shipping Charter Party Form for carriage of coal outwards to Danube, Rosario, R. Parana and Uruguay.

Wharfage. Dues paid for the use of a wharf.

Wharfinger. The person in charge of a wharf.

Windward. That side of a ship facing the quarter from which the wind blows.

Wireless Installation Inspection Certificate. Certificate issued by the Board of Trade to the effect that the annual survey has shown the wireless equipment to be in good order.

W.N.A. Winter North Atlantic marking of the loading grid.

Working Day. A period of time during which it is recognized that work shall be carried out, *e.g.* in British ports an eight hour day is customary whilst in some countries abroad the hours may be as many as ten each day. If a charter party provides for six working days for loading, and work is continuous throughout the day and night, one calendar day may be calculated according to the terms as three working days, *e.g.* 24 hours = three 8 hr. days.

W.p. Without prejudice. An expression used in the offer or acceptance of a settlement of a claim by agreement to denote that the offer or acceptance is made provided that it does not prejudice the rights of the parties in the immediate or subsequent circumstances.

Y

Y.A.R. York/Antwerp Rules. Code of rules for the uniform adjustment of general average. These rules are acceptable by most maritime nations.

Yellow Flag. Flag flown by vessel entering a port requesting pratique and indicating that the vessel is free from infection.